WORSHIP PIANO

THE COMPLETE GUIDE WITH AUDIO!

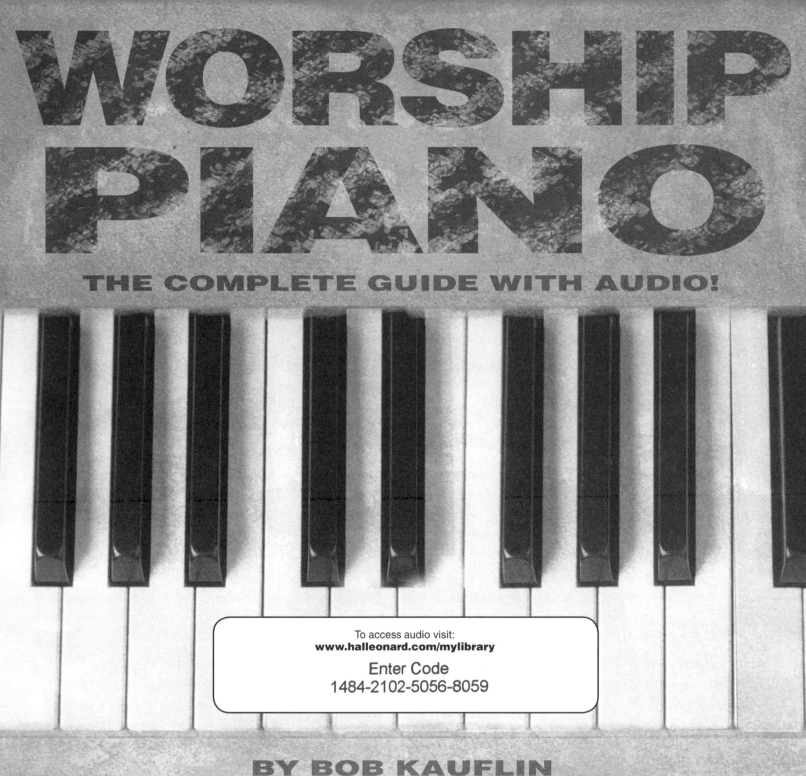

To access audio visit:
www.halleonard.com/mylibrary

Enter Code
1484-2102-5056-8059

BY BOB KAUFLIN

ISBN 978-1-4234-2968-5

HAL•LEONARD®

7777 W. Bluemound Rd. P.O. Box 13819 Milwaukee, WI 53213

In Australia Contact:
Hal Leonard Australia Pty. Ltd.
4 Lentara Court
Cheltenham, Victoria, 3192 Australia
Email: ausadmin@halleonard.com.au

Visit Hal Leonard Online at
www.halleonard.com

T0019128

INTRODUCTION

"Shout for joy in the Lord, O you righteous!
Praise befits the upright. Give thanks to the LORD with the lyre;
make melody to him with the harp of ten strings! Sing to him a new song;
play skillfully on the strings, with loud shouts." (Psalm 33:1–3, ESV®)

For centuries, pianists have been seeking to "play skillfully" as they accompany the church in singing God's praise. In recent decades, however, the pianist's role has evolved significantly. The changes have far surpassed any previous era in terms of what has changed and how quickly things have developed.

In the mid-20th century, the piano was used in the church primarily to accompany hymns and choirs, or for solo performances. Most pianists had developed note-reading skills in formal lessons. Playing by ear, or without notes, was the domain of secular pop, jazz and rock music. In many small churches (and even some large ones), the piano was at the center of what was happening musically. Not anymore. A massive overhaul in church music occurred with the Jesus Movement of the late '60s and early '70s. Note reading gave way to the simple chords of rock and folk music.

On the bright side, an entire generation of young musicians suddenly realized they could use their gifts in the church. At the same time, note-reading pianists were increasingly pushed to the fringes of the music ensemble as they agonized over the "music" they were now being asked to play. Notes, dynamic markings, tempo indicators and clear directions were replaced with chord names and confusion. Somehow, they were supposed to know what rhythms, voicings and melodies to play.

Decades later, classically trained pianists are still trying to figure out how to fit in with a band made up of drums, bass and guitar—all of whom are typically playing by ear. If you've picked up this book, you're most likely one of the thousands of note-reading pianists struggling to make sense of chord charts. For years, I've wanted to put something substantive together that would enable pianists to make the transition. When Hal Leonard approached me about writing a book on that topic, I jumped at the opportunity.

The good news is that what you're going to learn in this book will be less technically challenging than what you've been playing. You'll become better at playing less while contributing more. You'll learn how to play in the right places by listening to others. Most importantly, you'll discover how to play in ways that are emotionally engaging and help people "feel the truth" in the lyrics they're singing.

The purpose of this book is to teach you that skillful playing involves more than just playing the right notes. It's about playing what best fits the occasion. I've met more than one classically trained pianist who views playing by ear as an inferior form of music. It's not. It's simply a different one, and it actually takes a significant amount of practice to become skillful at it. As you add playing by ear to your musical toolbox, you'll experience the freedom and joy of developing a piano part that serves both the congregation you're leading and the musicians playing with you.

ABOUT THE AUTHOR

Bob Kauflin is a pastor, songwriter, worship leader and author with over forty years of experience in the church. He graduated from Temple University with a degree in piano performance, and then spent eight years traveling and writing for the Christian band GLAD. After serving as a pastor for twelve years, he became Director of Sovereign Grace Music in 1997. He oversees their album production and teaches on congregational worship through WorshipGod conferences, seminars and his blog, worshipmatters.com. His first book, *Worship Matters: Leading Others to Encounter the Greatness of God*, was published by Crossway in 2008, and his second book, *True Worshipers: Seeking What Matters to God*, was released in 2015. He and his wife, Julie, have six children and an ever-growing number of grandchildren.

CONTENTS

Page

1 The Keyboardist's Contribution 4

2 Reading Chord Charts 5

3 Common Chord Types 8

4 Playing Chords with Both Hands 11

5 Right-Hand Inversions 13

6 Slash Chords 16

7 Color Tones 19

8 More Slash Chords 23

9 Voicing 27

10 Nashville Numbering System 29

11 Rhythm and Feel 32

12 Thinking About Melody 40

13 Playing with Other Instruments 44

14 The Left Hand 48

15 Modernizing Hymns 53

16 Introductions 57

17 Turnarounds 60

18 Endings 63

19 Transitions 65

20 Incorporating Dynamics 67

21 Putting It All Together 72

22 Playing Behind Someone Speaking 75

23 Modulating 77

24 Acoustic Piano vs. Electronic Keyboard 81

25 Practicing 84

Appendix: Listening List 86

Chapter 1

THE KEYBOARDIST'S CONTRIBUTION

The keyboardist's primary contributions to a worship band can be summed up in four words: harmony, rhythm, melody and dynamics.

Harmony

Harmony describes the combination of notes that form chords to support the melody. Classically trained pianists play harmonies that are written out in advance, with no surprises. A keyboardist who leads worship in song has a wide number of harmonic options when considering how to support a melody or play with a band. We'll explore them together in the pages to come.

Rhythm

In a band setting, the piano is part of the rhythm section—usually made up of percussion, bass, guitar and piano. As the name implies, one of the primary functions of this group of instruments is to provide rhythm. This includes tempo as well as "feel" (more on that later). A solo keyboardist playing by ear will fill in some of what the missing instruments would add.

Melody

Every song has a melody, but playing the actual tune of a song is only one of your options. You can also play melodic fills between vocal lines or counter melodies that occur during the song. Note-reading pianists tend to play the vocal melody of every song. As we'll see, that's not necessary, and can even be unhelpful.

Dynamics

One of the common mistakes pianists make is playing everything (rhythm, melody and harmony) at the same volume. This tends to make their playing sound mechanical and monotone. I'll suggest helpful ways to incorporate dynamics in your playing.

These four contributions to a band's sound aren't equally important and won't always be utilized in a keyboard part. Sometimes your job will be to simply provide harmonic color. Other times, you'll be playing a creative melody. On other occasions, you'll emphasize the rhythmic feel of a song. Dynamics are important, regardless of what you're playing, but in some contexts it will be more significant than others.

Chapter 2

READING CHORD CHARTS

Before we look at chords and the different ways you can play them, we need to talk about something that can strike fear in the heart of a note-reading pianist: *the chord chart*. Chord charts are a form of musical shorthand that only give you the basic guidelines you need to play a song. Your job is to supply the details.

In a church context, chord charts vary in the amount of detail they provide. Downloaded charts from some sites give you loads of information, while other sites only give you lyrics and chords (and you can't always be sure those are even correct).

Here's an example of a simple chord chart using the first verse of John Newton's hymn, "Amazing Grace." We'll use the key of E because, well, a lot of guitarists like that key!

```
     E              A     E
A - mazing grace, how sweet the sound
     E                 B
That saved a wretch like me
   E              A     E
I once was lost, but now am found
     A       B    E
Was blind but now I see
```

The first thing you might notice is that the "music" (although some classical musicians would hesitate to use that term) is a bit incomplete. It begs multiple questions that printed music would readily answer.

- What's the time signature?
- Where's the key signature?
- What's the melody?
- What notes do you play?
- When do you play them?
- What rhythmic patterns should you use?
- What's the structure of the song?

In others words, a note-reading pianist can feel completely lost when handed a chord chart. Here are some tips that will help guide you:

Time Signature

Chord charts will sometimes indicate the time signature at the top of the page. If not, you can figure it out by singing the song. If you don't know the song, you'll have to ask someone or wait until you hear it. (I'm assuming you're familiar with "Amazing Grace" and know the time signature is 3/4.)

Key Signature

Again, you'll often see something like "Key of E" at the top of the chord chart. If not, the key is usually either the first or the last chord on the chart. Often it's both, which is the case here. If you're not sure, playing through the song should give you an idea of what key it's in. If all else fails, ask another musician.

Melody

Unless you're playing from a lead sheet, it's assumed that you either know the melody already or will pick it up fairly quickly!

Notes

Chord charts communicate which notes to play through *chord symbols*. These are generally placed directly above the lyric syllables they're to be played over. (If your chord chart is sloppy, that may not be the case.)

A chord symbol tells you two things:

1. The **root**, or lowest note of the chord.

2. The **type** of chord (major, minor, etc.)

Not all chords are created equal. The combination of letters and numbers after a chord name, called the *extension*, tells you which notes to play. If you don't see an extension after a chord name, it's typically a major chord. The chords shown above are major chords, made up of a major third interval topped by a minor third interval. (If you're unsure what that means, we'll talk more about chord types in Chapter 3.)

Timing

As I mentioned earlier, good chord charts place the chord symbols above the syllables they're to be played over. Sometimes a chord chart will include bar lines, or even slashes to mark the beats. Most often, however, you'll just get chord symbols. No need to panic! The chords are played when the syllables are sung. In the previous "Amazing Grace" example, the first E chord is played over the syllable "maz" in the word "amazing." You don't need to change chords until you sing the word "sweet." The next chord change comes with the word "sound." So, even though there are no bar lines, the melody of the song informs you that the first E chord lasts for two bars, while the A and the next E are each played for one bar.

Rhythmic Patterns

We'll discuss this more fully in Chapter 11. Rhythmic patterns are determined by the style of song you're playing, who's playing with you, and what they're playing. For now, just know that you almost never need to play as much rhythmically as you think you do!

Song Structure

Chord charts sometimes include the structure (section order) of the song at the top of the page. It might look something like this:

INTRO - VS1 - PRE - CH - TURN - VS2 - PRE - CH - TURN - BR - CH - CH - TAG

Charts may also indicate the song sections to the left of the lyrics, like this example from "Jesus Paid It All" (Hall/Grape):

     C   **G**   **C**
VS1   I hear the Savior say, "Thy strength indeed is small.

         C   **Am**   **Dm**   **G**   **C**
       Child of weakness, watch and pray, find in Me thine all in all."

     C   **Am** **C**   **G**
CH   Jesus paid it all,   all to Him I owe.

     C   **F**   **Dm**   **G**   **C**
     Sin had left a crimson stain, He washed it white as snow.

Here's what's going on:

INTRO   The introduction. If this isn't written out, you have to come up with your own. More on that later...

VS1   Verse 1. Not much more to say.

PRE   The pre-chorus, sometimes called the "lift." This section is different from the verse and leads into the chorus. Not all songs include a pre-chorus, and it's typically brief.

CH   The chorus or refrain.

TURN   The turnaround, which is instrumental music that connects different sections of the song.

BR   The bridge, which adds lyrical and musical interest to the song (hopefully).

TAG   Also called the outro. This is a musical idea used to end the song. It may or may not include lyrics, and it sometimes mirrors the intro.

This might sound very complicated, but it's not unlike the musical ideas found in a classical sonata (exposition, development, recapitulation, coda). Depending on your leader, the song structure will either be spelled out in advance, or you'll have to be alert to your leader's direction during the song.

Enough of me talking. Now it's your turn to participate. In each chapter of this book, you'll have opportunities to put what you've learned into practice. Here's the first one:

 Try playing the chords of "Amazing Grace" (page 5) while singing it. Don't worry about how your voice sounds. There are good reasons to sing while you play, which we'll discuss later. For now, you can play each chord in root position. If you're not sure how to play any of the chords, keep reading and come back to it.

Chapter 3
COMMON CHORD TYPES

A chord is usually defined as at least three notes played together, although a chord can be implied by two notes, or even one! I've known more than a few classically trained musicians who don't have a clue what chords they're playing in a song. If you have a weak foundation in music theory, you might be one of them!

So, let's begin with some chord theory. I'm assuming you have a basic knowledge of scales. If you don't, take some time to get familiar with scales in the common keys (C, D, E, F, G, A, B♭). Hal Leonard's *Master Scale & Chord Guide for Keyboard* is a great resource if you need to brush up (HL00240525).

While there are over 30 chords in every key we could look at, we're only going to focus on the chords you'll most likely play in a worship band context. We want to not only develop a knowledge of which notes constitute a chord, but also what those notes actually sound like and feel like to play.

In its most basic form, every chord is made of musical intervals stacked on top of each other. When we talk later about different ways of playing chords, you'll see that, although the notes remain the same, the actual intervals can vary widely.

Major (written as Cmaj, CM, or more commonly, just C)

A major chord consists of two intervals: a major third topped by a minor third. The distance from the root to the top note is a perfect 5th. Play the chords below and notice the cheerful, solid sound. I've written note names for the first two examples, and you can fill in the rest. Refer to the notated chords below if you get stuck. *Note: If your chord theory is weak, don't skip over this section!*

1. C - E - G
2. D - F♯ - A
3. E - ___ - ___
4. F - A - ___
5. ___ - B - D
6. A - ___ - ___
7. B♭ - ___ - F

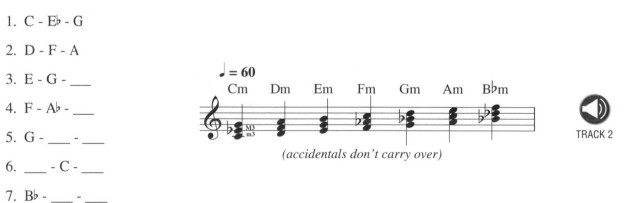

♩ = 60

C   D   E   F   G   A   B♭

(accidentals don't carry over)

TRACK 1

Minor (written as Cmin, Cm, or C-)

A minor chord contains a minor third topped by a major third. Notice the sad, reflective sound as you play these chords.

1. C - E♭ - G
2. D - F - A
3. E - G - ___
4. F - A♭ - ___
5. G - ___ - ___
6. ___ - C - ___
7. B♭ - ___ - ___

♩ = 60

Cm   Dm   Em   Fm   Gm   Am   B♭m

(accidentals don't carry over)

TRACK 2

Dominant 7th (written as C7)

Three intervals are needed to make this chord: a major third topped by two minor thirds. It's called a dominant 7th because a chord built on the fifth scale tone of any key is called the "dominant." The sound of this chord tends to pull towards the root (tonic) chord, although it can stand on its own. The example below begins with a G7 chord, which is the dominant 7th chord in the key of C.

1. G - B - D - F

2. A - C♯ - ___ - G

3. B - D♯ - ___ - A

4. C - E - ___ - B♭

5. D - ___ - ___ - C

6. ___ - G♯ - B - ___

7. F - ___ - ___ - E♭

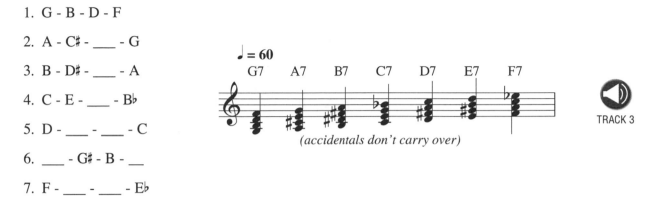

(accidentals don't carry over)

TRACK 3

Minor 7th (written as Cmin7, Cm7, or C-7)

This chord also contains three intervals: a minor third topped by a major third, topped by another minor third. As the name suggests, the distance between the root and the top note is a minor 7th. It has a plaintive or melancholy sound.

1. C - E♭ - G - B♭

2. D - F - ___ - C

3. E - G - ___ - D

4. F - A♭ - ___ - E♭

5. G - ___ - ___ - F

6. ___ - C - E - ___

7. B♭ - ___ - ___ - A♭

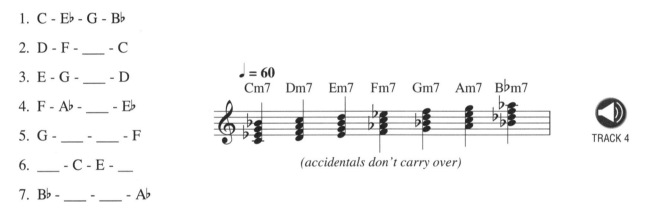

(accidentals don't carry over)

TRACK 4

Suspended (written as Csus4, Csus, or occasionally C4)

Two intervals form this chord: a perfect fourth topped by a major second. It often resolves to a major or minor chord, but it can also stand on its own.

1. C - F - G

2. D - ___ - A

3. E - A - ___

4. F - ___ - ___

5. G - ___ - ___

6. A - ___ - E

7. B♭ - E♭ - ___

(accidentals don't carry over)

TRACK 5

9

Diminished (written as Cdim or C°)

This chord is built with a minor third topped by another minor third. It isn't common in modern worship music, but it occasionally makes an appearance in hymns such as "Great Is Thy Faithfulness" (Chisholm/Runyan). See if you can identify this chord by its ominous and foreboding sound, due to the outward notes forming a tritone.

1. C - E♭ - G♭

2. D - F - ___

3. E - ___ - B♭

4. F - A♭ - ___

5. ___ - B♭ - ___

6. A - ___ - ___

7. B♭ - ___ - F♭ (E)

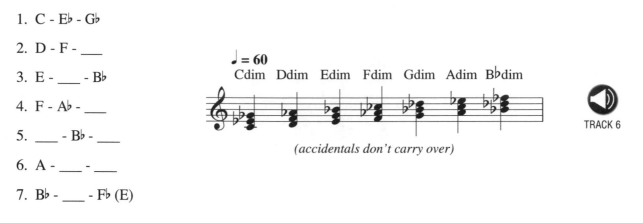

(accidentals don't carry over)

TRACK 6

Augmented (written as C+ or Caug)

A major third topped by another major third forms an augmented chord. Contemporary worship songs don't use this chord much, but one example is "Let My Words Be Few" by Matt and Beth Redman. It also has a foreboding sound, with an added element of anticipation.

1. C - E - G♯

2. D - F♯ - A♯

3. E - ___ - B♯ (C)

4. F - A - ___

5. ___ - ___ - D♯

6. A - ___ - E♯ (F)

7. B♭ - D - ___

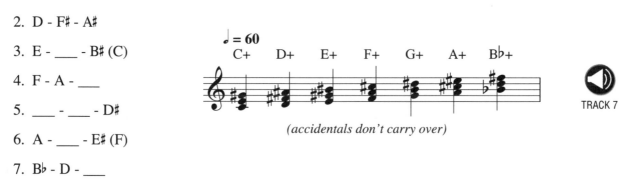

(accidentals don't carry over)

TRACK 7

You might not agree with the adjectives I've used to describe these chords. That's okay. The point is to have some sense in your mind of what they sound like. That will help immensely as you learn to play by ear.

 Play through all the chords we just studied while saying their names, either internally or out loud.

Chapter 4

PLAYING CHORDS WITH BOTH HANDS

Up to this point, we've played each chord in root position with the right hand. When adding the left hand, many classical pianists will simply play the root note and leave the right hand in root position, like this:

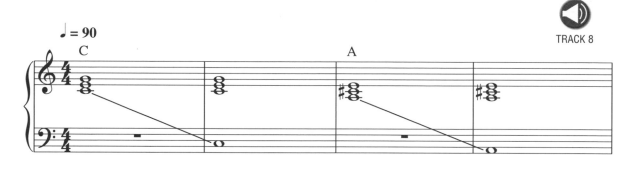

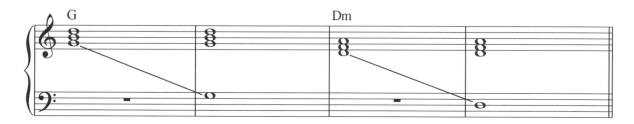

If you're going to play chord charts well and sensitively, however, you need to take advantage of *all* the ways a chord can be played.

New sounds emerge when we rearrange the right-hand notes, sometimes doubling the bass (root) note. Listen to how these chords sound different when you arrange the right-hand notes in various ways.

Let's take this one step further by playing two notes in the left hand and two notes in the right hand. In each two-bar phrase, you're playing the same chord four different ways.

When you play a three-note chord with four notes, one of the notes is going to be doubled. In the previous example, we doubled either the root or fifth of the chord, rather than the third. Doubling the third isn't necessarily wrong, but the sound is slightly unbalanced.

 Try playing the chord positions we just explored in as many keys as you can. Remember that you're playing the same chord each time, but spreading the notes across both hands. Get a feel for what each chord sounds like. It will serve you immensely as you progress through this course.

 Here's another chart of "Amazing Grace" in the key of E, with a couple of different chords. Play through it again, this time splitting the chords between both hands. For now, just play and hold each chord until the next chord change. Then try playing it in the key of F, using the second chart. It will help you keep time if you sing the hymn as you play.

E	**A**	**E**

A - mazing grace, how sweet the sound

E	**B**

That saved a wretch like me

E	**E7**	**A**	**E**

I once was lost, but now am found

C♯m7	**B**	**E**

Was blind but now I see

F	**B♭**	**F**

A - mazing grace, how sweet the sound

F	**C**

That saved a wretch like me

F	**F7**	**B♭**	**F**

I once was lost, but now am found

Dm7	**C**	**F**

Was blind but now I see

Chapter 5

RIGHT-HAND INVERSIONS

By dividing chords between two hands, we've inadvertently wandered into the territory of *inversions* (actually, that was my plan). An inversion is formed by rearranging the notes of the chord. In **first inversion**, the bottom note moves up an octave to the top.

first-inversion chords

To form a **second inversion** chord, take the bottom note of the first inversion chord and put it on top. You can also think of second inversion as taking the two bottom notes of the original root-position chord and moving them on top.

second-inversion chords

The number of possible inversions for a chord always equals the number of notes in the chord minus one. A three-note chord has two inversions, a four-note chord has three inversions, etc.

Here are some examples of four-note inversions for the right hand. Notice that you don't have to play all four notes of the chord in the right hand because you're already playing the root note with your left hand.

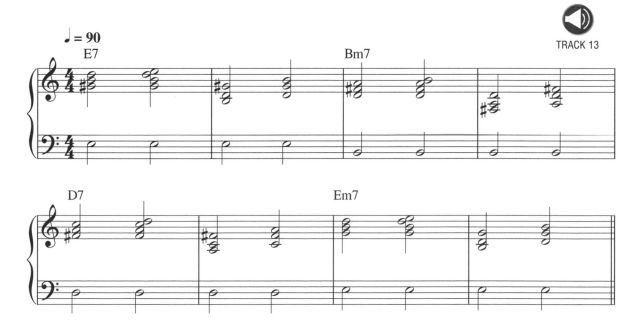

Inversions can be played by one hand, or spread across both hands. In the previous example, your left hand always played the root while your right hand played the chord inversions. But you can also play the lowest note of the inversion in your left hand. We'll study that in the next chapter.

Learning to use right-hand inversions is more than simply being creative. They help you play more musically. Here are three reasons why:

RIGHT-HAND INVERSIONS

1. Enable you to minimize note movement between chords, making your playing less choppy.

2. Make it easier to shape a melody with the top notes of your chords.

3. Give you the option of using different textures for different songs and sections of a song.

Here's how that might work when playing "Amazing Grace":

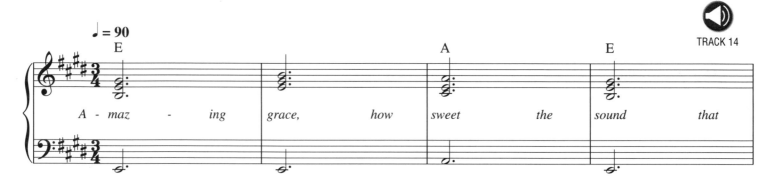

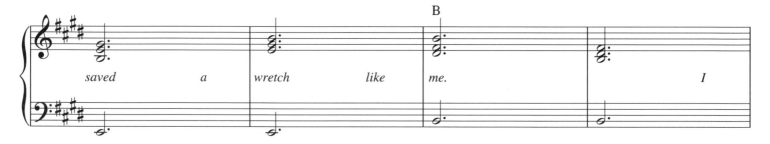

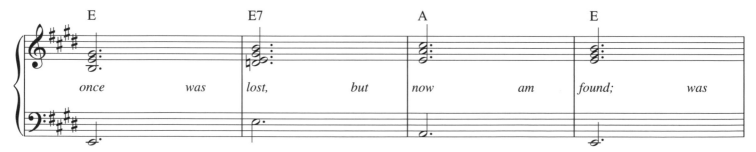

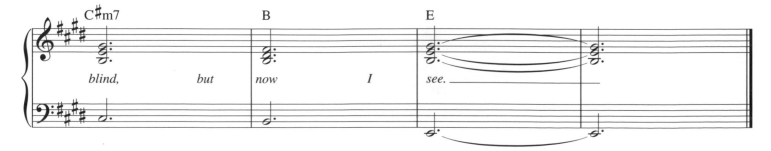

Try playing "Amazing Grace" in the key of F, using various inversions in the right hand.

 Practice the following series of common chords in each key until you're comfortable with both the feel and the sound.

The progression used below is **I – IV – V – vi – ii7 – V – I**. Capital Roman numerals indicate major chords, while lowercase numerals are for minor chords.

TRACK 15

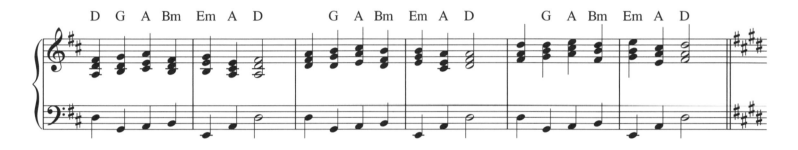

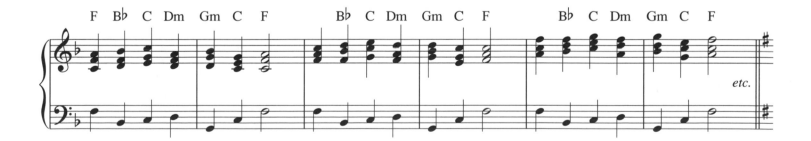

Chapter 6
SLASH CHORDS

Up until this point, we've played all the two-hand chords in root position. That means the lowest left-hand note is the name of the chord. Many more options exist, however.

The chord inversions we've been playing in the right hand can also be spread across both hands. In chord charts, these are typically notated as *slash chords*.

> *A slash chord shows two symbols side-by-side, separated by a forward slash.*
>
> *The first part tells you which chord to play in your right hand.*
>
> *The second part tells you what the lowest note in your left hand should be.*

The first slash chord we'll look at is the first inversion of a chord. Again, it's produced by moving the root note up an octave, so the third of the chord becomes the bottom note. A chord written "C/E" is pronounced "C over E." Here are some examples of how slash chords are written:

C/E   =   E in the left hand and a C major chord in the right hand

E/G♯   =   G♯ in the left hand and an E major chord in the right hand

Fm/A♭   =   A♭ in the left hand and an F minor chord in the right hand

Here's how they sound:

First-inversion slash chords sound a little more pleasing by removing the doubled third in the right hand, as shown here:

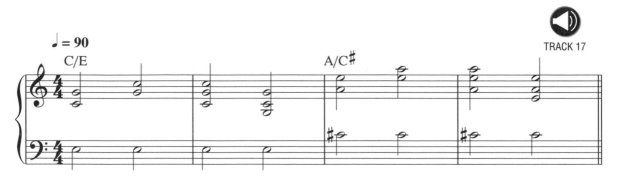

Here are two minor chords played in first inversion, without the doubled third:

TRACK 18

A second-inversion slash chord is formed by using the fifth of the chord as the bottom note.

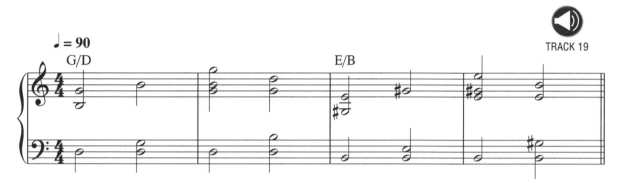

TRACK 19

There are numerous options at your disposal when playing inversions. In order to get more comfortable playing chord charts, it's good to become familiar with the sound and feel of various chords (you'll hear me say that a lot). The following exercises will help you develop these skills.

YOUR TURN Practice playing different inversions of common chords in major keys. I've notated two here to get you started.

YOUR TURN Practice using inversions of these common chords in minor keys:

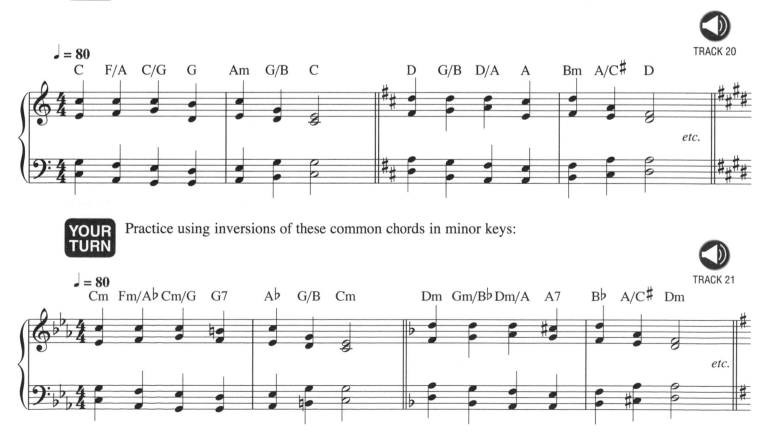

TRACK 20

TRACK 21

17

Practice playing arpeggiated inversions of major chords (continue in the keys of G, A and B♭):

TRACK 22

Practice playing arpeggiated inversions of minor chords (continue in the keys of Em, F♯m and Gm):

TRACK 23

You'll learn other types of slash chords in Chapter 8.

Chapter 7
COLOR TONES

Color tones are notes we add to a chord that aren't part of the basic chord. It's kind of like making a mistake, only it isn't.

Chords become more interesting and creative when color tones are used. Of course, if you're playing with other musicians, you need to make sure that the notes you're adding don't conflict with what they're playing.

Color tones are sometimes written in the chord name, but they don't have to be. You can add them to a chord whenever it seems appropriate. In this book, sometimes I include the color tone in the chord symbol, but not always. Here's a rundown of four color tones you can experiment with:

Add2 (written Cadd2 or C2)

This is the most common and adaptable of all the color tones. You simply add the second note of the scale to the chord. It adds richness to the harmonic sound, and it won't get in the way of someone else's playing. It works well with both major and minor chords. You can hear the difference below.

TRACK 24

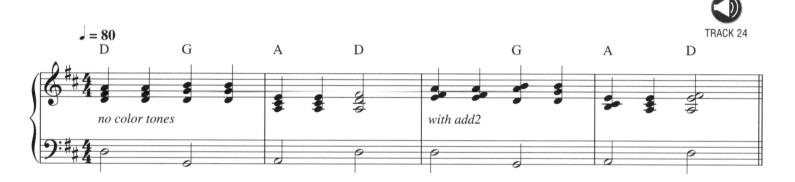

YOUR TURN The following exercise uses the add2 color tone in various inversions. I've written it in E and F, but try playing it in other keys, too.

TRACK 25

You can also add the second to a chord without playing the third. This is sometimes labeled "sus2," but you can use it anytime you see "2" in the chord name. When all four notes are played (add2), the sound is richer and more dense. When you omit the third (sus2), the sound is spacious and more ambiguous. Here's a progression that could accompany the verse of "Here I Am to Worship" by Tim Hughes:

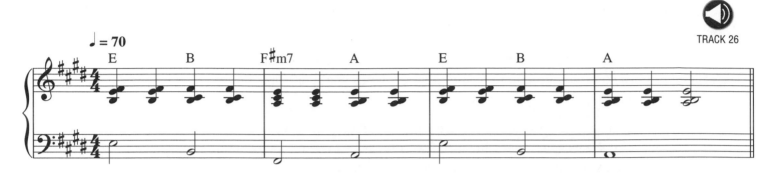

TRACK 26

Add4 (written Cadd4 or C+4. If you see just C4, it usually means Csus)

You can add this color tone to either a major or minor chord. When added to a major chord, the sound is dissonant and dense. A minor chord with an added fourth is still dissonant, but less so. This works well when you're playing the dominant chord (or "5 chord") of the scale. In the next example, a fourth has been added to the D chords.

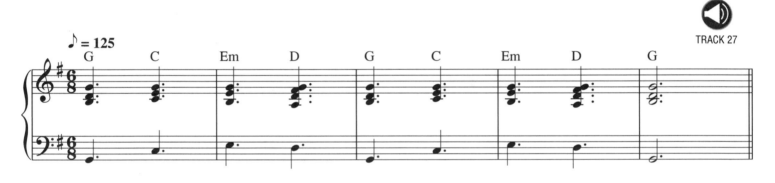

TRACK 27

Here's the same idea, adding a fourth to the Dm7 and Gm7 chords.

TRACK 28

For notational purposes, the fourth added to a minor 7 chord can be written two ways: Dm7+4 or Csus/D. The second chord is the same as the first, but it's written as a slash chord that might be easier for pianists (and guitarists) to understand.

Add6 (written C6)

This color tone is less common, but it can be used to introduce ambiguity to the sound. I've added it to the circled chords below. (I've also included a few other color tones we've been studying.)

TRACK 29

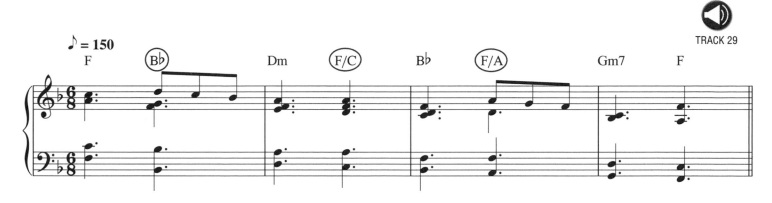

Major 7th (written Cmaj7 or C△7)

The major 7th tone adds a "bitter sweetness" to a major chord. While it can be played at the top of the chord, the major 7th tone is typically played next to the root note. The circled chords in this example show how you might use a major 7th chord in the beginning of "Holy, Holy, Holy" (Tune: NICAEA).

TRACK 30

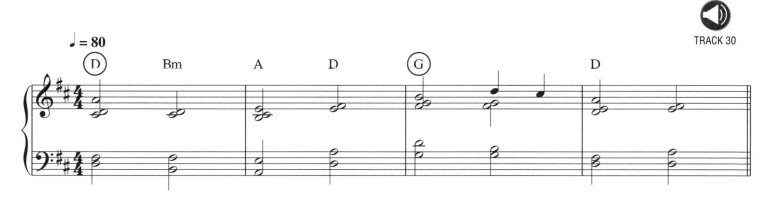

 YOUR TURN Here's an exercise that uses various inversions of the major 7th chord. I've written them out in C and D, but see if you can play them in other keys, too.

TRACK 31

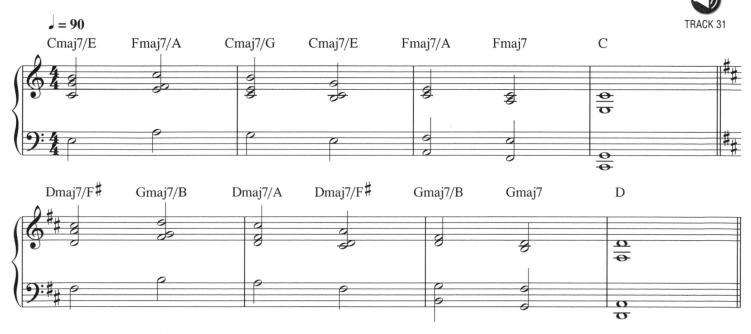

21

With so many options for color tones, it can be a bit overwhelming to figure out which ones to use (and when). In general, color tones will be part of the key you're playing in. When playing a G chord in the key of C, for example, you can use a 2nd (A), 4th (C) and 6th (E). A Gmaj7 chord would include an F♯, which isn't in the key of C.

Here's a chart to help you quickly determine which color tones can be used in the chords built on the first six tones of a major scale (in this case, C).

	Add2	Add4	Add6	Maj7
C maj (I)	✓	✓	✓	✓
D min (ii)	✓	✓	✓	
E min (iii)	✓	✓		
F maj (IV)	✓		✓	✓
G maj (V)	✓	✓	✓	
A min (vi)	✓	✓		

 Try adding color tones to the chords of "Amazing Grace" in the keys of E and F. Play through it several times, experimenting with which color tones work and which ones don't. As you practice new techniques, keep in mind that you'll use them less frequently when you're playing on a Sunday.

```
     E              A     E
A - mazing grace, how sweet the sound

     E              B
That saved a wretch like me

  E     E7    A     E
I once was lost, but now am found

     C♯m7  B    E
Was blind but now I see
```

```
     F              B♭    F
A - mazing grace, how sweet the sound

     F              C
That saved a wretch like me

  F     F7    B♭    F
I once was lost, but now am found

     Dm7   C    F
Was blind but now I see
```

Chapter 8

MORE SLASH CHORDS

The slash chords we looked at earlier have one thing in common. The root note has always been a part of the chord in the right hand. Slash chords, however, can also have a root note that *isn't* included in the chord. Here are four examples:

The Flat 7 Slash Chord

Our first irregular slash chord has a bass note in the left hand and a major chord in the right hand built on the flatted 7th scale tone of that note. It's often used as a IV/V chord that leads to the tonic. In that case, it's called a "4 over 5." Here are a few examples:

F/G	=	G in the left hand and an F major chord in the right hand
D/E	=	E in the left hand and a D major chord in the right hand
B♭/C	=	C in the left hand and a B♭ major chord in the right hand

Occasionally, you'll see this written as an 11 chord. That's because when the right-hand chord is played in tonic position, its top note is the 11th tone of the root scale. In modern chord notation, however, they're nearly always written as slash chords.

$$\text{F/G} = \text{G}^{11} \qquad \text{D/E} = \text{E}^{11} \qquad \text{B♭/C} = \text{C}^{11}$$

 YOUR TURN Practice the ♭7 slash chords below. Take time to familiarize yourself with how they sound and feel. What you learn in this book will have little impact unless you begin to trust your ears and fingers more than your eyes.

Let's add a few ♭7 slash chords to "Amazing Grace" in the keys of E and F.

E   **D/E**   **A**   **E**
A - mazing grace, how sweet the sound

    E   **A/B**   **B**
That saved a wretch like me

  E   **D/E**   **A**   **E**
I once was lost, but now am found

    C♯m7 **A/B** **B** **E**
Was blind but now I   see

      F   **E♭/F**   **B♭**   **F**
A - mazing grace, how sweet the sound

     F   **B♭/C** **C**
That saved a wretch like me

  F   **E♭/F**   **B♭**   **F**
I once was lost, but now am found

   Dm7   **B♭/C** **C** **F**
Was blind but now I   see

The Major 9 Slash Chord

Another common slash chord is made up of a bass note in the left hand and a major chord in the right hand built on the 5th scale tone of that note. Here are some examples:

A/D   =   D in the left hand and an A major chord in the right hand

D/G   =   G in the left hand and a D major chord in the right hand

B/E   =   E in the left hand and a B major chord in the right hand

Although I'm calling this a slash chord, it's typically written as a major 9 chord, since the top note of the right-hand chord, when played in tonic position, is the 9th scale tone of the bass note.

$$A/D = Dmaj^9 \qquad D/G = Gmaj^9 \qquad B/E = Emaj^9$$

I'm including it as a slash chord because it's difficult to play in root position with one hand.

YOUR TURN Here's an exercise to learn the sound and feel of the major 9 chord. Notice that each two-bar phrase contains the same chord labeled two different ways.

TRACK 33

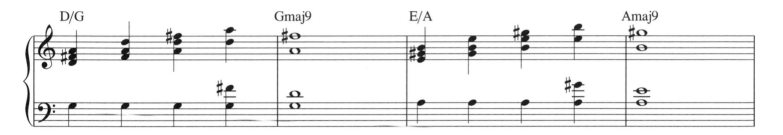

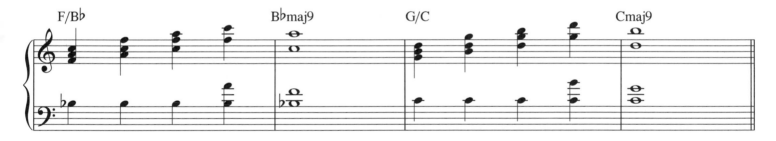

 YOUR TURN In this chromatic exercise, you'll play a major 9 slash chord in every key.

TRACK 34

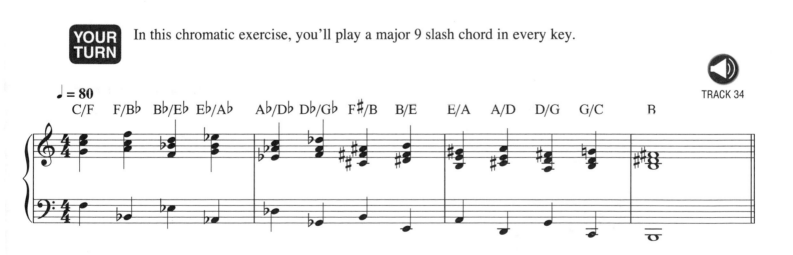

The Supertonic Slash Chord

This chord is often used as a passing chord. It's composed of a bass note in the left hand and a major chord in the right hand built on the 2nd scale tone of that note. Here are some examples:

G/F   =   F in the left hand and a G major chord in the right hand

E/D   =   D in the left hand and an E major chord in the right hand

A/G   =   G in the left hand and an A major chord in the right hand

The next two exercises will help you become familiar with the sound and feel of the supertonic slash chord.

TRACK 35

TRACK 36

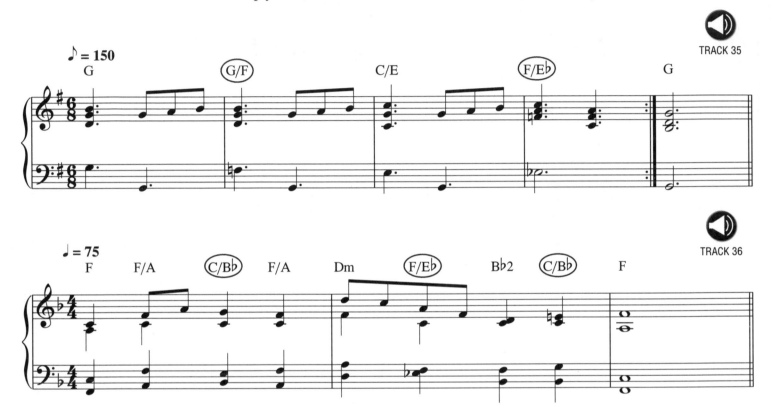

The Half-Diminished Slash Chord

There's one more slash chord I want to mention, simply because you might run into it on a chord chart. It's commonly referred to as a half-diminished chord, or a "minor 7 flat 5." Here's how it can be written:

$C^{\o 7}$ = C half dim7 = Cm7♭5

I'm calling this a slash chord because it can also be written as E♭m/C, meaning an E♭ minor chord in the right hand over a C in the left hand. It's typically used as a substitute for the minor 2 chord, which leads to the dominant 7 chord and then the tonic. Here's how it sounds:

TRACK 37

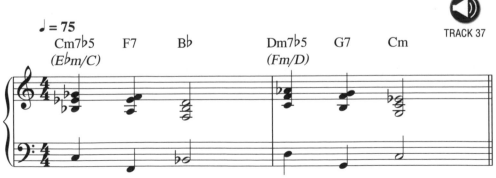

Chapter 9
VOICING

The term "voicing" describes how you combine your knowledge of chords, color tones and inversions to play chords.

As we've seen, there are many ways to play a single chord. With so many options, you might wonder what drives your decisions. Here are four aspects to consider:

Lyrics

Good voicing enables you to shape chords that support the lyrics. When leading a congregation, we're never simply playing music. We're using music for its ultimate purpose—to direct people's hearts and minds to the Giver of all good gifts (James 1:17). We're told in Colossians 3:16 that the songs we sing should enable the word of Christ to dwell in us richly. That means we should play in a way that encourages people to focus on the lyrics—not us, or even the music.

One of the best ways to develop a sensitivity to the lyrics is to sing when you play. You don't even need a microphone. Singing as you play accomplishes a number of important things. It makes you more aware of the words you're singing, helps you play in a way that serves the lyrics, tells the congregation that you're there to support what they're doing, and communicates that the words we sing matter.

> *Sing when you play.*
>
> *If that doesn't come naturally to you, practice singing at home.*

Melody

By changing the position of chords, we can shape melodies with them. We can introduce melodic elements that complement and support the vocal melody, rather than simply playing block chords. We'll explore this concept in Chapter 12.

Other Instrumentalists

When you're playing with a band, good voicing plays an important role. We'll talk more about this in Chapter 13, but essentially, you should voice your chords to stay out of the way of other instruments that are playing in the same part of the audio spectrum.

Variety

Changing up the chord voicings can help people hear lyrics in a fresh and meaningful way, which is why we do what we do. Voicing makes the difference between a pianist who plays predetermined, predictable chord patterns and one who plays *musically*.

Here's a chart for the chorus of "Jesus Paid It All" (Hall/Grape). See how many voicings you can come up with using the techniques you've learned so far. Play the song slowly enough to feel secure about the voicings you're choosing. Try not to alter too many chords in one pass.

A   F#m   A   E
Jesus paid it all,   all to Him I owe

A   D   A/E   E   A
Sin had left a crimson stain; He washed it white as snow

 Incorporate color tones into the following verse of "Holy, Holy, Holy." (I've included some slash chords for practice.)

D   Bm A   D   G   D
Holy, holy, ho - ly, Lord God Al - mighty

A   Bm7 E/G# A   A/E   E   G/A   A
Early in the morn   -   ing our song shall rise to Thee

D   Bm A   D   G   D
Holy, holy, ho - ly, merciful and mighty

Bm D/F#   G   D   G   A   D
God   in three Per - sons, blessed Trini - ty

 Try playing this accompaniment for the chorus of Helen Lemmel's hymn, "Turn Your Eyes Upon Jesus." It incorporates some of the color tones and slash chords we've looked at, which are notated in the chord symbols. Try to use voicing that minimizes the movement from chord to chord and highlights a melodic progression.

F2   C2/E   Dm2   Cm7+4
Turn your eyes upon Je - sus

**   Bb2   Gm7   Csus   C/Bb**
Look full in His wonderful face

**   F2/A   F7   Bbmaj9   Bbm7**
And the things of earth will grow strangely dim

**   F/C   Bb/C   C7   F2**
In the light of His glory   and   grace

28

Chapter 10
NASHVILLE NUMBERING SYSTEM

This is a good place to introduce what is known as the "Nashville Numbering System." For centuries, musicians used Roman numerals to indicate chords, rather than letter names. If you studied theory as a classical pianist, you're probably familiar with them. In the 1950s, a man named Neil Matthews developed a simpler way of identifying chords based on Arabic numerals. It later became known as the Nashville Numbering System (NNS).

The NNS replaces the letter names of a scale with numbers that correspond to their position in the scale.

Notice that the NNS doesn't use accidentals. The numbers correspond to the note in the scale, which is major unless otherwise indicated.

When used to indicate chords, the numbers represent letter names. A single number typically indicates the chord that starts on that note *in a major scale,* unless the song is in a minor key. For example, in the key of C:

Am   F   C   G   C   would be written: 6m   4   1   5   1

To avoid confusion, numbers will often include extensions to indicate exactly what type of chord should be played. Here are some examples in the key of C:

Dm   =   2– or 2m

Am7   =   6m7 or 6–7

Bdim   =   7dim or 7°

Slash chords function the same way they do with letter names. Again, in the key of C:

F/G   =   4/5

Am/G   =   6m/5

B♭/C   =   ♭7/1

In the above example, notice that if the root of the chord isn't in the scale, an accidental is placed to the left of the number.

A single number generally lasts a whole measure. If the chords change within a measure, a line is drawn underneath the chords to indicate they occur within the same bar.

Key of C:

4/4   <u>2m   5</u>   1 = Dm / G / |C

4/4   <u>6m   4</u>   1 = Am / F / |C

A number with a diamond or a circle around it (or above it) means you should play the chord once and let it ring until the next chord.

Why Use the Nashville Numbering System?

There are several reasons that people use the NNS for chord charts:

Easier to communicate

This is why the NNS was developed in the first place. If musicians are playing in different keys (due to capos or tuning), you can use the same chord numbers for everyone.

Easier to transpose

The greatest benefit of the NNS is that it makes transposing a song so much easier. A song can be played in any key without changing the chart. Software programs exist now that can automatically transpose your chord charts. But if you don't have access to them, you have to reenter all the chord names every time you want to write a chart in a different key. You can avoid that by using numbers from the beginning. A chart that uses the NNS might be played by the keyboardist in B♭, while the guitarist is capoing up one fret and playing it in A.

Easier to understand chord relationships

The NNS also trains you to hear how chords relate to the key you're in. For example, a C major chord sounds different in the key of G as a 4 chord, in the key of F as a 5 chord, and in the key of D as a ♭7 chord.

Easier to hear harmonic patterns

A chord is rarely played in isolation. As you grow in your understanding of the scale tones chords are based upon, you'll begin to hear patterns and be able to transpose more easily. For instance, a 6m - 4 - 1 progression will use *different chords* in different keys, but it will still be the *same progression*. Even if you don't play from NNS charts, it's good to understand the concept and know the scale numbers of the chords you're playing.

Develop your understanding of the Nashville Numbering System by writing in the correct chords for each key. I've filled in the first row to get you started.

	6m	4	1	5	2m	3m	4	5	1
C	Am	F	C	G	Dm	Em	F	G	C
D									
E									
F									
G									
A									
B♭									

 Play the above progression in each key using some of the color tones you've learned. For deeper study, play the progression in 4/4, 3/4, and 6/8 (not simultaneously, though!)

 Play "Amazing Grace" in the keys of D, G, and A with the Nashville Numbering System.

1   **4**   **1**
A - mazing grace, how sweet the sound

  6m   **2M**   **5** **5/4**
That saved a wretch like me

1/3   **1⁷** **4**   **1/3**
I once was lost, but now am found

  2m7 **5** **4/1**   **1**
Was blind but now I see

Convert a few of your church's chord charts to the NNS by adding numbers next to the chords. That way, if you're ever asked to transpose one of them on the fly, you'll be ready!

Chapter 11
RHYTHM AND FEEL

Up until this point, we've focused on how a keyboardist can serve congregational singing through **harmony**. We're now going to explore **rhythm**.

One of the primary changes that occurred in church music during the '70s was the introduction of drums and bass. Drummers (or percussionists) and bass players work together to provide a foundational rhythm that the other musicians build upon. A good bass player will be locked into what the kick drum is playing, in terms of both the tempo/feel and the rhythms. For that reason, it's a good idea to always be listening to what the kick drum and bass are playing.

Drums and bass aren't the only instruments that provide rhythm. Acoustic and electric guitars—and yes, keyboard—can also contribute rhythmically to songs. Unless you're playing alone, a keyboardist's main job isn't typically to create the rhythmic feel. It's essential, however, to be aware of and locked into the rhythm that the drummer or another musician has set.

> *If you play with a drummer and bass player,*
> *always be listening and locking into what they're doing.*

There's a difference between keeping time and playing with feel. If a drummer or percussionist simply keeps time, it can sound unmusical. He/she isn't contributing much more than a metronome, click track or drum loop would.

That's why the rhythmic element that drums provide is often described as *groove* or *feel*. You can think of it as a "metronome with heart." Groove is based on time, but it's not overly strict. Different notes receive different accents. In some songs, a drummer might play ahead of the beat, while other songs might call for playing behind the beat. Playing ahead of the beat tends to push the song along, while playing behind the beat brings a sense of relaxation and solidity. Most good drummers tend to play ever so slightly behind the beat.

Typically, playing with groove or feel isn't a strength for note-reading pianists. So, we'll start slowly and work through the various components of playing with feel.

Whole and Half Notes

Most worship songs have fewer chord changes than traditional hymns (which makes them more appealing to guitar players). If the chords change on the downbeat, a keyboardist can simply play whole or half notes with each chord change. In 3/4 or 6/8 meter, you'd play dotted half or dotted quarter notes.

At first, you might feel terribly uncomfortable leaving so much space in your playing. But remember that other members of the band provide rhythm, too. Your job is to support the feel they're providing. Even if you're a solo pianist, the melody the congregation sings can provide enough rhythm to move the song along.

Play and sing the hymn "Praise to the Lord, the Almighty" in 3/4 meter (Tune: LOBE DEN HERREN), but only play on the downbeats when the chord changes. Otherwise, let the chords ring. I've added barlines to help you keep track of where you are in the song. Feel free to use any of the voicings we've covered in previous lessons.

F | | B♭ | |C |F
Praise to the Lord, the Al - mighty, the King of cre - a - tion

F | | B♭ | |C |F
O my soul, praise Him, for He is thy health and sal - va - tion

F/A | B♭ | Dm | |C
All ye who hear,   now to His temple draw near

F/A | B♭ |C |F
Join me in glad ado - ra - tion

You'll remember (I hope!) that when you play from a basic chord chart, the timing of the chords is determined by the *lyrics*, not barlines. So, even if two chords are written close together (as they are over the word "creation"), they're played when the syllable beneath them is sung. In this case, both chords last three beats.

 Here's a chart for the hymn "When I Survey the Wondrous Cross" in 4/4 meter (Tune: HAMBURG). In this exercise, start each line with a whole note, and then play two half notes. Try to minimize your hand movement by using inversions in your right hand.

E |A   E
When I survey the wondrous cross

E |C♯m B
On which the Prince of glory died

E |A   E
My richest gain I count but loss

E |B   E
And pour contempt on all my pride

Quarter Notes

When playing whole notes, you're contributing primarily to the harmony of a song, although you should still be aware of the feel that the drummer or another musician has set up. You can add a rhythmic element by playing quarter notes. Generally, quarter-note patterns are played in the right hand, while the left plays half or whole notes. This style is often used in slower songs or ballads.

With a quarter-note pattern, your mind should be focused in two places. First, you should be listening to (or even better, *singing*) the melody of the song and seeking to support it. Second, you should be listening to the kick drum and bass (if they're playing) to make sure you're in sync with what they're doing.

Here's a quarter-note pattern that would work for "Revelation Song" by Jennie Lee Riddle:

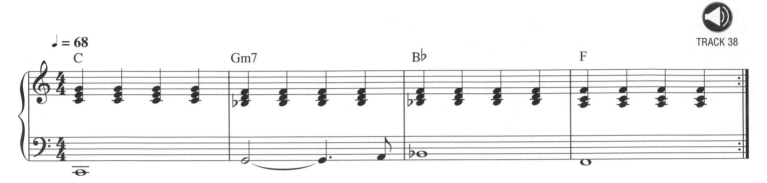

The following accompaniment could be used during the verse of "Majesty (Here I Am)" by Martin Smith and Stuart Garrard:

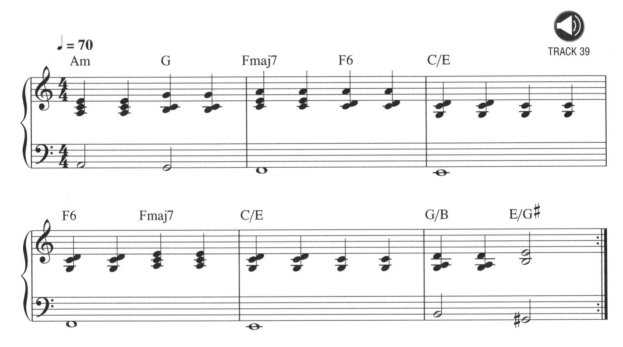

 YOUR TURN Use the chords below to accompany the first verse of the hymn, "It Is Well with My Soul" (Spafford/Bliss). Play quarter notes in the right hand, as indicated by the slashes.

Bb / / / / I Gm / / / / I Cm / F / I Bb / F/A /

Gm / / / / I C7 / / / / I F / / / / I F7 / / /

Bb/D / / / / I Eb / / / I C/E / C / I F / / /

Bb/D / Eb / I Bb/F / F / I Bb / Bbsus / I Bb

Rocking 8ths

You can contribute even more significantly to the rhythm by using rocking 8ths. Again, this is typically used in slower songs. In the next two examples, notice how we're using different inversions in the right hand to minimize movement.

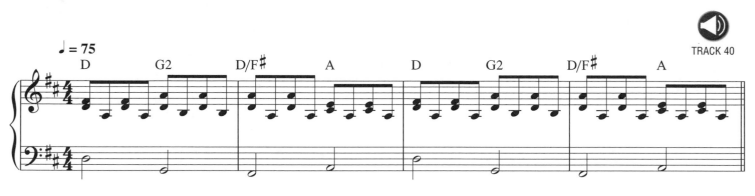

Notice in the second example that we added a rhythmic element to the left hand to support the chords.

YOUR TURN Play the chords below with rocking 8ths to accompany the first verse and chorus of "Mighty to Save" (Fielding/Morgan). This chart is in the key of G, but it begins on the 4 chord.

Verse:

C | G | Em | D

C | G | Em | D | C   D | C   D

Chorus:

G | D | C   G | Em   D

G | D | C   G | Em   D

Rocking 8ths Variation

You can also alternate the 8th-note pattern between hands as you play. The following example could accompany the verse of "You Are My King (Amazing Love)" by Billy Foote.

TRACK 42

YOUR TURN Experiment with different forms of a rocking 8th pattern for the following chart of "Holy, Holy, Holy." Try to vary the inversions you use in your right hand. You can also practice this hymn using a combination of half notes and rocking 8ths.

C   Am G   C   F   C
Holy, holy, ho - ly! Lord God Almighty

G/B   Am   G   G/D   D7   Gsus   G
Early in the morn - ing our song shall rise to Thee

C   Am G   C   F   C
Holy, holy, ho - ly! Merciful and mighty

Am Em   F   C   Dm   G   C
God in three Per-sons, blessed Trini - ty

Guitar Style (Nashville Triplet)

Guitarists use a variety of rhythmic strum patterns, but one of the most common is what I simply call "guitar style," also known as a "Nashville triplet." It looks like this:

If you're playing with an acoustic guitarist, there's no need to duplicate what the guitar is doing rhythmically. But if you don't have a guitarist, this pattern can provide a rhythmic groove and a sense of momentum without overplaying. It works best in 4/4 meter and often sounds better if you omit the third of the chord.

The simplest form of the guitar style leaves out the second accented chord in each measure. Here's an example of what I mean. This pattern would work for the first verse of "Open the Eyes of My Heart" by Paul Baloche.

TRACK 43

Notice that you can vary the voicing even when the chord remains the same. Here's another version of the same idea, with a slightly more active left hand. This could be used to accompany the chorus of "This Is Amazing Grace" (Wickham/Farro/Riddle).

TRACK 44

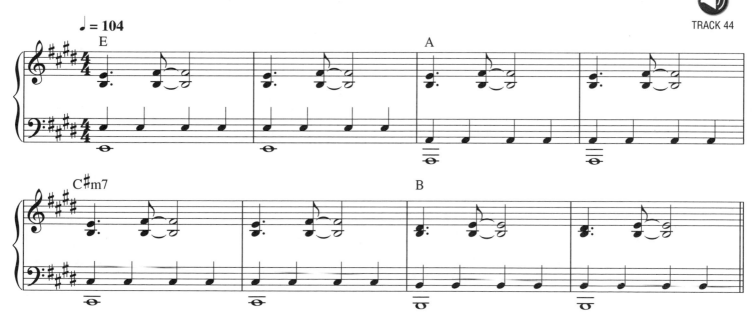

The following example shows a fuller version of the guitar style that could work during the chorus of "How Great Is Our God" (Tomlin/Reeves/Cash).

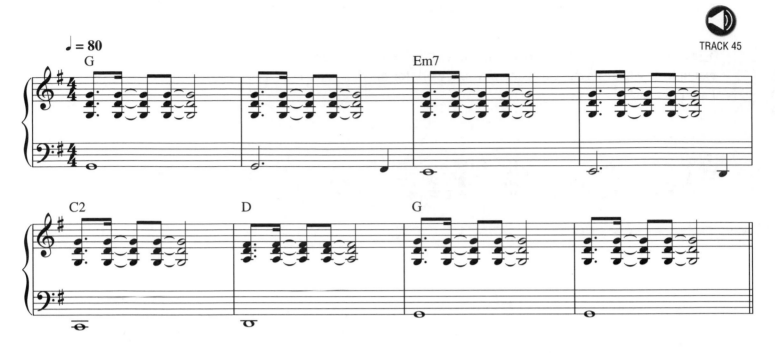

Notice that you didn't have to change the right hand part in bars 1–5, even though you played three different chords (G, Em7, C2). That's the benefit of using color tones and arranging your voicings to minimize harmonic movement. Notice also that bars 2 and 4 use a passing tone in the bass to connect the bars more smoothly.

Of course, a guitar style doesn't have to be played in block chords. You can communicate the same rhythmic effect with single notes, like this:

 Try using your own voicings for the above progression, with chords or single notes in the right hand.

We've covered at least five different ways of adding rhythmic feel to a song. As you're getting used to them, it's helpful to play a similar pattern for a whole verse or chorus, or even a whole song. Once you become more familiar with your options, you'll be able to make better musical choices. With practice, you'll almost automatically know what to play when you hear a song. You'll understand that certain styles, patterns and voicings fit some songs better than others.

So, how do we make decisions about what to play? I'm glad you asked!

What Guides Our Musical Choices?

Having 88 keys and 10 fingers can make our musical options seem endless, but a church musician has a unique call and responsibility that performers outside the church don't have to answer to. Church musicians are called to be servants. "As each has received a gift, use it to serve one another, as good stewards of God's varied grace" (1 Peter 4:10, ESV). We have considerations that go beyond simply playing what we *can* play or *like* to play.

How do we make decisions about what to play? We addressed this partially in Chapter 9, but here are three more ways to think about what we do, all revolving around our role as servants.

Serve the song.

The lyrics to a worship song are the most important aspect of that song. The music matters as well, but its role is to complement the truth of the lyrics. As I mentioned earlier, we're to let "the word of Christ" (not musical experiences) dwell in us richly when we sing. That means I don't want to play anything that's distracting or that might overpower the lyrics. I want to use styles and voicings appropriate to the lyrics being sung. For example, I wouldn't choose soft arpeggios to accompany "A Mighty Fortress Is Our God," or bombastic chords to accompany "Silent Night."

Serve the other musicians.

When playing with a band, I need to realize that I'm not the only one making sound. That's why it's important to be able to hear the other musicians, whether that's through in-ear monitors, wedges, or their amps. If someone else in the band is covering the rhythm, harmony or melody, I should complement (not duplicate) what they're doing. We'll discuss this more in Chapter 13.

Serve the congregation.

More than once, I've visited a church where the musicians played creative arrangements. Their skill was impressive, but a large part of the congregation wasn't singing. That's because the band's playing left no room for the congregation to sing. The arrangements drew more attention to the musicians than the song itself. As a result, people were either trying to keep up with the melody or simply watching.

For some musicians, it's a significant paradigm shift to consider how what they play will affect the people they're leading.

Our playing can either encourage people's participation or hinder it.

Chapter 12

THINKING ABOUT MELODY

Note-reading pianists often assume that "melody" refers only to the vocal melody of a song. While that's an important place to start, it's only one aspect of it. Melody also comes into play with transitions, turnarounds, intros and counter-melodies. In other words, it's more than just playing the tune of the song.

So, how should we think about "melody" when playing by ear? First, make sure you know the melody of the song you're seeking to accompany. While the song melody isn't the only melody to be concerned about, it is the most important one. If you're going to complement the melody, you have to know what it actually is.

Second, don't assume you need to play the melody. Playing the melody of a song is not only unnecessary; at times, it's unhelpful. Contemporary worship songs often have syncopated melodies that sound stilted and wooden when played on a keyboard (e.g. "Open the Eyes of My Heart," "How Great Is Our God," "This Is Amazing Grace"). So, it's unwise to simply play the melody on the piano.

Third, rather than crowding or obscuring the melody, learn how to complement and support it. Here are some approaches you can take:

Let the song melody speak for itself.

Use chords to emphasize downbeats or chord changes, rather than melodic patterns. If the song is familiar, the congregation will do fine with the melody. What they need to know from the musicians is the key, the meter, and when to start singing. We'll talk about how to create effective introductions in Chapter 16.

Play portions of the melody when the tune is unfamiliar.

When introducing a new song, it can serve the congregation well to play the melody in a higher octave so it's clear. At times, I've realized the people don't seem to know the melody, so I'll start playing it in the second verse.

Play a melody during a turnaround.

As long as the guitarist or solo instrument isn't already functioning in this way, the keyboardist can play a distinct melody that ties the song together during instrumental breaks between song sections. These breaks are often called "turnarounds" or "turns." This melody might be played as octaves, two-note intervals, or even single notes. We'll spend more time on this in Chapter 17.

It brings a greater cohesiveness to a song when you play the same melody for each turn. Here are three examples of what you could play in a turnaround that uses a common 1 - 4 - 6 - 5 progression.

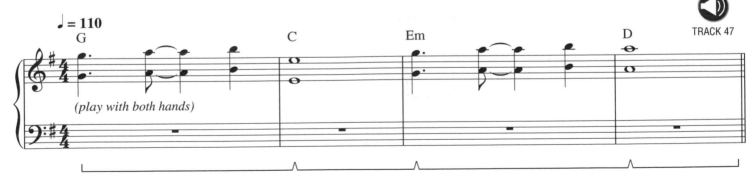

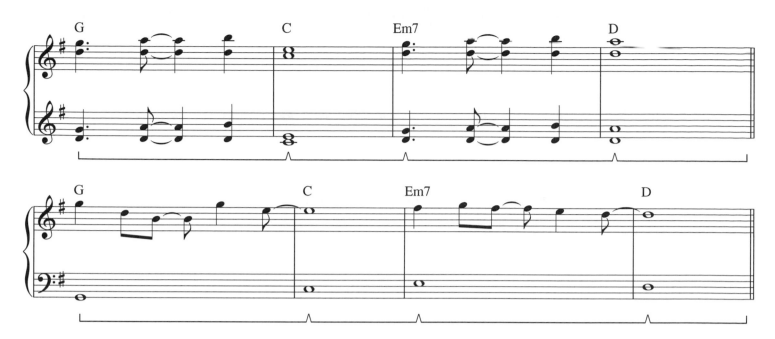

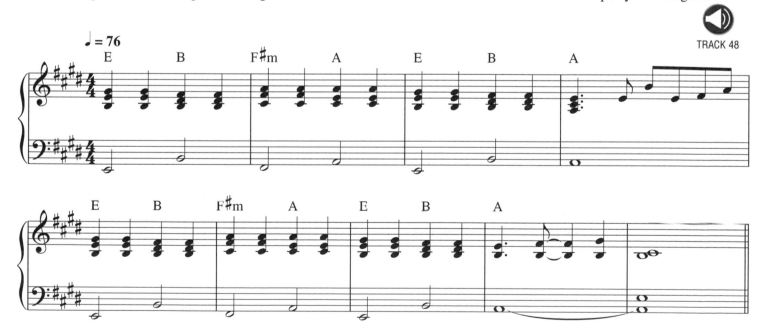

In the first example, you didn't play anything in the lower register of the keyboard. If you're playing with a band, that's often the better choice because it's more difficult for lower melodies to cut through the sound of the other instruments. (Also, did you notice the add2 color tone in measure 3 of the third example?)

 Try coming up with your own melody using the chord progression in the previous examples.

Play a melody between phrases of a song.

One of the most common places to add a melodic element is between the vocal phrases of a song. This is something you should do selectively—considering not only the song, but also what the other instruments are doing. Here's an example of adding a "fill" in the middle of the verse of "Here I Am to Worship" by Tim Hughes:

Notice how the quarter-note pattern stops just before the fill in bar 4, to help set it apart. The fill in bars 8 and 9 helps move the song toward the chorus.

Try coming up with your own chord pattern and melodic fill for "Here I Am to Worship." It can be simpler than the one in the previous example. Try to hear in your head what you're going to play before you play it.

It's better for your playing to be simple and confident than complex and unsure.

Play a melody that repeats or expands the melody of the song.

It can be difficult for note-reading pianists to create melodic lines on the spot. A quick way to get started is to echo part of the melody, or to expand on it. Here's an example that would work for the verse of "How Great Is Our God" (Tomlin/Reeves/Cash).

TRACK 49

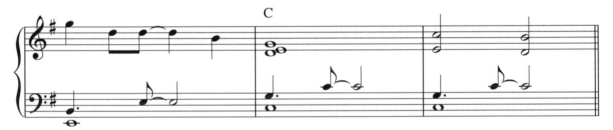

Here are a few things to note about this example:

- We added a color tone in measures 1 and 5.

- The left hand is providing rhythm through a simplified guitar feel.

- The piano melody "answers" the melody of the song, rather than playing on top of it.

 Using the example above, try coming up with your own melody in bars 2 and 4.

Play a melody that complements the melody of the song.

You can play a melodic motif over the tune of a song as long as it doesn't distract from what people are singing. That melody can be played by itself, but can also be the highest note of the chords you're playing.

The following example could work with the chorus of "10,000 Reasons (Bless the Lord)" by Jonas Myrin and Matt Redman:

TRACK 50

Notice how I used the highest note of each chord to create a new melody. Most likely, I'd play something simpler, but this gives you an idea of what's possible.

Three Things to Remember about Melodic Fills

1. Play in time.

Playing a fill out of rhythm takes something away from the song rather than adding to it, which can be a distraction.

2. Don't conflict with what other instruments are playing.

Regardless of your monitor system, make sure that you can hear the other instruments. If you have an electric guitarist who plays leads, a solo instrument like a violin, or a synthesizer player who also plays melodic fills, your opportunities to serve in that way will be limited.

3. Hear in your head what you're going to play before you play it.

As you grow in your ability to play by ear, it's a good habit to try to hear in your mind what you're going to play before you actually play it. When you practice, try humming a fill before playing it. Hearing what you're going to play becomes easier as you practice. Really.

Chapter 13
PLAYING WITH OTHER INSTRUMENTS

It's time to talk more intentionally about playing with a band. Some of these points also apply when you're playing by yourself, but they're even more important when you have other instruments to consider.

Pay attention to what other instruments are playing.

The first rule of thumb when playing with other musicians is to make sure you can hear them! How you do that largely depends on the kind of monitor system you use. If you have the option of using stereo in-ear monitors, by all means do! Stereo allows you to spread out what you're hearing and makes each instrument more distinct. I've found it helpful to pan the instruments in the same way they're placed on the platform. If a guitar player is standing to my right, I'll pan the guitar over to the right. If you use wedges or foldback monitors, you'll have to factor in what other sounds you can hear. If you don't use monitors at all, make sure you consider where the amps are placed and which direction they're facing.

The most important thing is that you're able to hear the other musicians. There are several negative effects of not hearing the band well:

- You don't know whether or not you're playing in time.

- You can't tell if your fills are stepping on fills that others are playing.

- When you stop playing, it feels like the bottom drops out of the sound, so you'll be tempted to play more notes and more often.

- You'll make it harder for the person running the sound to mix the band in a way that makes you sound better and serves the congregation.

The more instruments are playing, the more important it is to determine how you can best fit in. Here are two important rules to consider when playing with others:

The 100% Rule

The total sound produced by the musicians adds up to 100%. The more players, the smaller the percentage you'll contribute. Now, that doesn't hold quite true because of the audio spectrum (which we'll get to shortly), how long notes are held, and other factors. But you can assume that if your band has eight musicians in it, you should be playing less than if it's just you and a guitarist.

The "Piece of the Pie" Rule

Similar to the 100% rule, think of the sound all the musicians make as the pie. The more musicians, the smaller your slice. "Less is more" is a popular phrase among musicians. It's popular because it's true! Unless a song specifically calls for you to play a lot of notes, the keyboard parts that contribute the most to your band's sound will have fewer notes than you're accustomed to playing.

Less is more. Really.

Be aware of the audio spectrum.

All the sounds we hear—loud, soft, beautiful, harsh, identifiable or confusing—are actually vibrating air. The slower the vibration, the lower the pitch of the sound. The faster the vibration, the higher the pitch. We measure vibrations in a unit called a Hertz (Hz), named after Heinrich Rudolph Hertz. He was the scientist who provided conclusive evidence that electromagnetic waves really exist. One Hz = one cycle per second. The audio spectrum is the name for the range of vibrations humans can hear, starting at zero and going past 20,000 (or 20 kHz).

This brief science lesson helps introduce the musical audio spectrum. Every instrument occupies a specific range of vibrations. Below is the general range of various instruments. (These show where the fundamental sounds lie, and don't include the overtones that can be produced.)

- Guitar: 80–880 Hz

- Electric Bass: 40–260 Hz

- Vocal: 110–660 Hz

- Violin: 200–3500 Hz

- **Piano: 27–4200 Hz**

- Kick drum: 60–100 Hz

- Snare drum: 110–5000 Hz

Most instruments fill a relatively narrow section of the audio spectrum. Pianos, however, are able to cover a wide range of tones. For this reason, in addition to thinking about *what* you play, it's also important to consider *where* you play. Notes played at the bottom, middle, and top of your keyboard produce very different results. Listen to the difference as you play a progression for the chorus of Matt Maher's "Lord, I Need You" in three different ranges.

TRACK 51

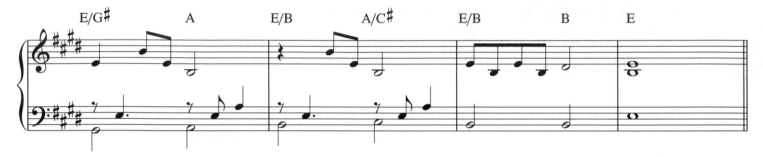

Notice how we added a rhythmic element in the left hand and a few color tones in the right hand. (In the high-range example, I probably wouldn't even play the left-hand notes.)

It's not necessarily wrong to play in the same audio range as other instruments. In fact, sometimes it's unavoidable. Here's the general rule to follow:

> ***If you're going to duplicate the sounds or rhythms of other instruments, make sure it's intentional.***

If you're playing the same thing another instrument is playing, the sound engineer will have to choose which one to bring up in the mix. If you're playing *exactly* what someone else is playing, that won't be a problem. But if you're slightly off, or your part is slightly different, hearing both at equal volume will only make the band sound messy (which obviously is not the goal).

Leave a hole in the middle.

Sometimes it's helpful to use a "doughnut" style. As the name implies, your left hand plays in the lower registers while your right hand plays in the higher registers, leaving a "hole" in the middle for other instruments and the congregation to fill.

Here's an example that could accompany the chorus of "Your Name" (Baloche/Packiam):

TRACK 54

As we've progressed through this book, have you noticed that you don't have to play every note in every chord? This is especially important when you're playing with other instruments that are filling in the harmonies. But it also applies when you're playing by yourself. Your job is to support the congregation, and the more notes you play, the more they might have to fight to be heard.

YOUR TURN Try playing doughnut-style with the following progressions:

Key of G

4/4   G | D | Em | C | G | D | Em | C | G ||

Key of D

3/4   D | A | G | D | D | A | Em | D ||

Know who's driving the song.

When the keyboard is the main instrument, I typically play more fully. If a guitar is leading the song, however, my role becomes supportive. I can play *a lot* less and shape what I play around what the guitar is playing. The primary instrument might change from one section of a song to another. For instance, you could have a secondary role during most of the song, but take the lead in the bridge, or perhaps the last chorus.

YOUR TURN Play the following progression in two different ways. First, as though you're the primary instrument, and then as if you're playing with a full band. Try using a guitar-style rhythm with a metronome marking of about ♩ = 110.

Key of D

4/4   D | G D | A | Bm G | D | G D | G A | D ||

Chapter 14
THE LEFT HAND

One of the most challenging areas for pianists (including me!) is how to use your left hand. In classical music, the left hand plays a crucial role and is equal in importance to the right hand. That's not the case for modern worship songs, especially when you're playing with a band. Here are a few reasons why:

- The bass player already has the bass notes covered.

- If the keyboard and bass are playing different notes in the lower registers, the sound gets muddy.

- When you play keyboard in the lower registers, it's harder for the person running the sound to bring you up in the mix.

At the end of this section, I'll encourage you once again to think carefully about whether or not to use your left hand. It's not as necessary as you might think!

That being said, there are times when using your left hand is helpful. It can fill out the sound, especially when you're playing by yourself. So, let's talk about left-hand philosophy.

We've already seen how the left hand can play whole or half notes to provide a harmonic foundation for songs. Here are a few more ideas about how to use your left hand effectively:

Play with or around the bass player.

If you want to ease into using your left hand less, learn exactly what the bass player is doing and duplicate it. You can also play a simplified version of what the bassist plays, such as only playing the left hand on the chord changes, rather than playing the actual bass pattern.

As you copy what the bassist plays (whether with your band or listening to a recording), you'll quickly see why doubling the bass part isn't always a good idea. Bass players can play with nuance that a keyboard doesn't have, and it can sometimes sound clunky on a keyboard.

Play like a bass player.

If you don't have a bass player, your left hand can fill that role. Use your left hand to accent chord changes and downbeats, provide a basic rhythm, or change the dynamics.

Octaves or single notes?

When you want to bring a strong, rhythmic drive to a song with the left hand, you have a number of options. Your left hand can play single notes, octaves, or a combination of the two. Use single notes for a lighter sound, octaves for a heavier feel, and a combination for a strong downbeat with a lighter pulse the rest of the measure. I find the last option to be the one I use most often.

Listen to the differences in the following examples. On the third line, emphasize the downbeats and play the quarter notes at a softer volume.

In place of a quarter-note pattern, you can also use a variation of a guitar-style rhythm in your left hand.

TRACK 56

In 6/8 meter, splitting up the bass octaves can be a good idea. Depending on the song, it may be wiser to simply play dotted half notes in the right hand, like this:

TRACK 57

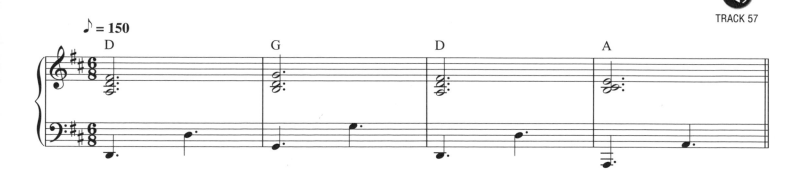

Here's a variation that produces a bigger sound. Make sure to pedal through each bar to get the full benefit of the bass notes.

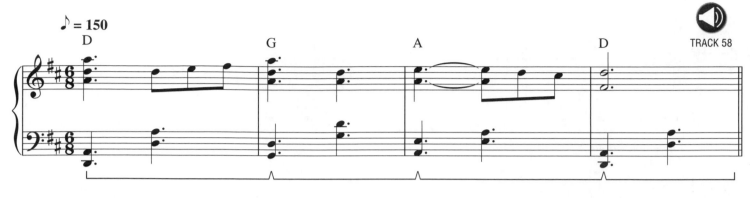

TRACK 58

 YOUR TURN Play through some songs that have a driving "four on the floor" beat. Possibilities include "This Is Amazing Grace," "Our God," "Hosanna (Praise Is Rising)," and "Blessed Be Your Name." Use different options for your left hand to get a sense of how they sound and feel.

Arpeggiate the chords.

When a song isn't driving, but you're playing more than whole/half notes, you can arpeggiate the left hand (play broken chords). Many note-reading pianists will naturally break chords up into arpeggios, but they often do it indiscriminately or erratically. This weakens both the sound and rhythmic feel. Using arpeggios intentionally can smooth out the sound and move a song along in the right ways.

You have several options when playing broken chords with your left hand. The simplest is the 1-5-8 arpeggio. (The numbers refer to scale tones.)

TRACK 59

Here are a few more choices:

The 1-5-10 arpeggio

TRACK 60

The 1-5-9 arpeggio, *à la* the chorus of "Stronger" (Fielding/Morgan)

TRACK 61

You can also continue the arpeggio with your right hand.

TRACK 62

Arpeggiated left-hand chords can also be used with inversions. Here's a reharmonization of the first half of "Amazing Grace" using broken chords in the left hand.

TRACK 63

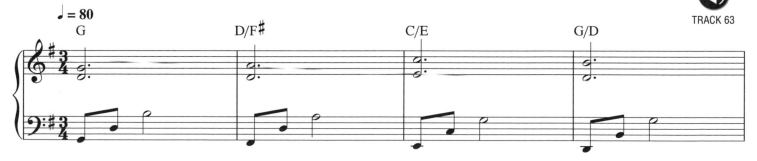

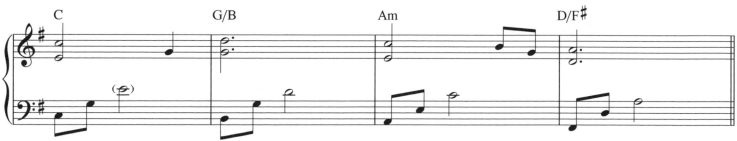

Your left hand can play a more substantive arpeggio using the 1-5-8-9-10 scale tones. The following accompaniment could work for the chorus of "Behold Our God" from Sovereign Grace Music.

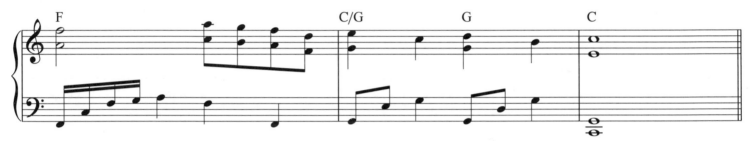

 The following exercise will help you get used to how arpeggiated chords feel in your left hand. Practice the progression in all the common keys, focusing on which chord you're playing as you play it.

Leave out the left hand.

We've looked at a few ways to use your left hand effectively in modern worship music. Keep in mind, though, that your best option might be to not use your left hand at all. Another approach is to keep your left hand above middle C. If you're in a band, make it a point to listen carefully to the kick drum and bass. This will help you make better choices about your left hand.

Chapter 15
MODERNIZING HYMNS

Psalm 98:1 exhorts us: "Oh sing to the LORD a new song, for he has done marvelous things! His right hand and his holy arm have worked salvation for him" (ESV).

Whenever God's people experience His saving power in a fresh and powerful way, the natural response is to sing a new song. But "new" doesn't always mean "never sung before." There are new ways of singing old songs that revive their meaning and impact for new generations. That's why one aspect of modern worship music I'm grateful for is a resurgence of traditional hymns that are theologically rich and proven over time.

Unfortunately, hymns don't always connect well musically and lyrically with younger generations. There are several reasons why:

- Hymns often have a different song structure than modern worship songs.

- Hymns can be wordy, leaving little space between phrases to breathe and think about the lyrics.

- The syllabic count of each phrase in a hymn is consistent from verse to verse, so the words can be used with multiple tunes. This characteristic is foreign to modern worship songs.

- Hymn lyrics generally require more thought to digest their meaning.

- Hymns are typically written in four-part harmony, so the chords stay the same in each verse. That means you can't use alternate harmonies to reflect the lyrics.

- The harmonic structure of hymns is often melody-driven and changes quickly, making it difficult for guitarists to play the chords.

For those reasons and more, hymns are often "modernized." Language is updated, melodies are rewritten, and harmonies are simplified. These changes don't necessarily make hymns *better*; just *different*.

That being said, there can be good reasons to play hymns in a modern style. (Since this is a book about playing piano and not songwriting, we'll assume the melodies remain intact.) One benefit is that you can introduce contemporary music styles to a traditional church without losing the gospel-driven, theologically substantive lyrics and time-tested melodies that are familiar to many people. Also, you can change harmonies to better reflect different emotions in different verses. Perhaps best of all, you're introducing new generations to lyrics and melodies that God's people have been singing for centuries.

So, if you're not simply reading out of the hymnal, how should you go about modernizing hymns? Here are a few suggestions:

Know the melody.

Because hymn melodies are often more dense than modern worship songs, it's especially important to know the melody. That will shape your choices, make it easier to harmonize, and prevent possible dissonances. Remember that your church most likely knows the hymn tune already, so you won't necessarily need to play it.

Simplify the chords.

The easiest way to modernize a hymn is to minimize the chord changes. While this was probably done initially to serve guitar players, simplifying the harmonies can also "open up" a hymn to make the lyrics and congregational singing more prominent.

Sometimes it works just to play chord changes on the downbeats of each measure. Often that will be the chord that's normally played there, but not always. Here's what this approach might sound like for the hymn "Be Thou My Vision" (Tune: SLANE).

TRACK 66

Notice how the right hand plays a counter melody that complements the melody of the hymn. I added a short fill at the end of bar 8, which is really all you need to move the song along.

We can simplify even further by using a repeating pattern in the right hand, usually built around open 5ths. This draws from what we learned earlier about color tones. Keep in mind that you don't have to play all the notes in a chord, and you can add color tones that aren't in the chord.

Here's an accompaniment for "Praise to the Lord, the Almighty" that combines some of the techniques you've learned so far. Notice the repeating pattern in the right hand.

Establish rhythmic and melodic patterns.

Another way to modernize a hymn is to add a rhythmic feel. The rhythm for hymns is typically supplied by the melody itself and isn't dependent on any rhythmic pattern other than the time signature. But groove and feel are characteristic of modern worship songs, and hymns can often (but not always!) be played to a groove or kick pattern.

The next example shows one way you could add a rhythmic element to the verse of "My Hope Is Built on Nothing Less" (Tune: SOLID ROCK). The left-hand syncopation creates a "2 against 3" feel.

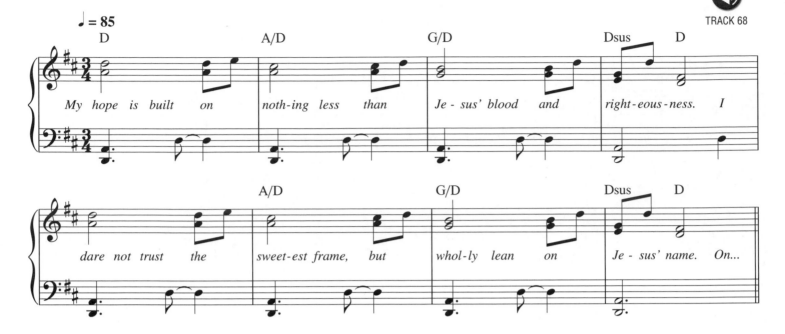

The next example uses a guitar style for the first 8 bars of "It Is Well with My Soul."

YOUR TURN Finish playing the verse of "It Is Well with My Soul" in guitar style, using the chart below.

B♭/D E♭   C/E   F
What - ever my lot, Thou hast taught me to say

B♭/D E♭ B♭/F F   B♭
It is well,   it is well   with my soul

Regardless of how you choose to modernize a hymn, remember that your goal is to serve the lyrics. Avoid coming up with a creative arrangement that has little to do with the words that are being sung. That has the unintended effect of encouraging people to focus more on the music than the truths they're singing.

Play what sounds good to your ear and is easy for the congregation to sing along with. You can develop your ear by listening to professional re-harmonizations of hymns and reproducing what's being played. Possible sources include Sovereign Grace Music, Indelible Grace Music, Passion Hymns and Page CVXI.

Chapter 16

INTRODUCTIONS

Whether it's a modern worship song or a hymn, you'll probably be asked at times to play the introduction for a song. If you're leading the music in your church, you'll do this a lot!

Pianists who play hymns are accustomed to playing the last few bars as an introduction, so everyone knows which hymn they're singing. In the more free-flowing environment of modern worship music, introductions are more varied.

A good introduction will alert the congregation to at least four things:

The tempo

Unless you're playing a freeform, ad lib introduction, it's helpful to establish a clear tempo in your introduction. That doesn't mean the intro has to be rigid, but the tempo should be clear enough for the congregation to know how fast or slow the song will be.

If you play with a click track or drum loop, the tempo is predetermined. If you have to come up with the tempo on your own, try singing the chorus in your head before you start. (If the song doesn't have a chorus, it's fine to use the beginning of the song.) This is another reason why it's good to be in the habit of singing while you play. You'll have a better idea of what the tempo should be.

The key

Some musicians enjoy playing introductions that are creative and complicated. It might be musically stimulating, but it doesn't help the congregation. A good introduction clearly communicates what key the song will be in.

When to start singing

A congregation isn't typically filled with trained musicians. Therefore, you need to be extra clear about when they're supposed to come in. This is often more of an issue with slower songs. In those cases, you can serve your congregation by slowing down slightly right before the singing starts. You can also change the volume, or even lift your head up and then bring it down. Ideally, your lead vocalist or band leader will help in this area.

Listen to the difference between this introduction for "The Power of the Cross" (Townend/Getty), first played straight and then with a slight ritard.

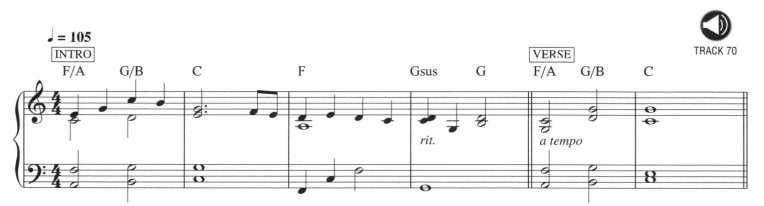

TRACK 70

The starting note

Good introductions not only communicate when the congregation should start singing, but also what the starting note is. If you've set up the tempo and key well, this isn't usually a problem. But, if there's any doubt about the congregation knowing what note to sing, it might be helpful to play a melody-driven introduction that's similar to what they'll be singing.

Keeping these principles in mind, you can build an effective introduction in a variety of ways, as shown in the next few examples.

The last chord progression of the song

Sometimes, simply playing the last melodic phrase of the chorus makes a great introduction. Here's an example using the last phrase of the hymn, "Crown Him with Many Crowns" (Tune: DIADEMATA).

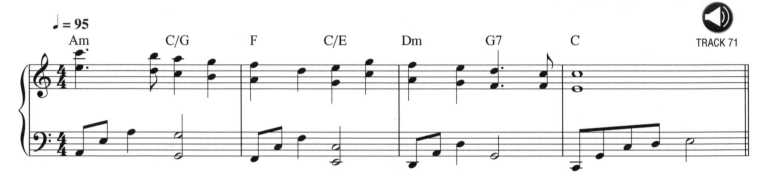

TRACK 71

The first chord progression of the song

You can build an introduction by playing the first phrase of the song—melodically, harmonically, or both. In the following example, we'll introduce the hymn "Come, Thou Fount of Every Blessing" (Tune: NETTLETON) by using the chords of the first four bars with a different melody.

TRACK 72

The turnaround

If you have a turnaround already mapped out on your chord chart, you can sometimes use that as the introduction as well. (We'll deal specifically with turnarounds in the next chapter.)

A single chord played in rhythm

Some hymns can be introduced simply by playing one chord in tempo. This works both for slow and fast songs. Here's a sample introduction for "When I Survey the Wondrous Cross" (Tune: HAMBURG):

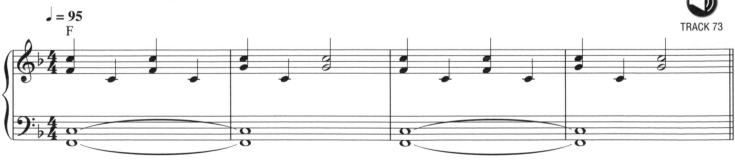

TRACK 73

The following introduction could be used for "This Is Amazing Grace" (Wickham/Farro/Riddle):

TRACK 74

A chord progression NOT found in the song

One of the most common introductions is a generic chord progression (also called a "vamp") that can be used for a variety of songs, and from which you can start a song quickly. The advantage is that you can shorten or lengthen it to serve the situation. You can also add a vamp after one of the other introductions we've talked about, to give a little "breathing room" before the song begins.

Here are some progressions you should get familiar with in all the common keys. All are in 4/4 time signature, but can easily be used for triple meters as well. (NNS numbers are included to help you transpose.)

KEY

	1	| 4/1				
D	D	| G/D				
	1	| 1sus				
G	G	| Gsus				
	1	4/1	| 1	4/1		
E	E	A/E	| E	A/E		
	1	| 4/1	| 5/1		| 4/1	
F	F	| B♭/F	| C/F		| B♭/F	
B♭	1	4/1	| 5/1	4/1		
	B♭	E♭/B♭	| F/B♭	E♭/B♭		
	6m	| 4	| 1	| 5		
C	Am	| F	| C	| G		
	1	| 6m	4			
A	A	| F♯m	D			

 YOUR TURN Use the above samples to play introductions for songs you're familiar with. Keep in mind that the introduction should be played in the same tempo and key of the song.

Chapter 17
TURNAROUNDS

A few years ago, I attended the Sunday gathering of a church that primarily sang traditional hymns. The voices carried the songs and there were few, if any, instrumental breaks between verses. The congregation sang robustly and the sound was beautiful.

But by the end of the service, I was exhausted. Not only were the hymns in higher keys than I was used to, but my voice never got to rest. My fatigue was partly due to the inherent differences between hymns and contemporary songs. But, because there were no musical interludes, I also had less time to reflect on the truths we were singing. I was reminded that instrumental breaks (or "links" as my UK friends would say) in congregational singing can be refreshing and provide an opportunity to think more deeply about the lyrics. They're standard for most modern worship songs.

Turnarounds (or "turns") are musical phrases that connect one section of a song to another. A turn might appear between a chorus and a verse, between two verses, between a verse and a bridge, or between a chorus and a tag.

If you're playing from a chord chart, the turn is often indicated on the chart. But churches being what they are (i.e. a group of volunteers), band members sometimes have to develop turns on their own.

Like introductions, turns can be drawn from part of the song, or you can create a new harmonic progression. You could start with some of the intros we looked at in the previous chapter. In addition, sometimes an effective turnaround is simply staying on a chord for an extra measure or two.

Following are some examples for songs in 4/4, 3/4 and 6/8.

Here's a possible turn for "Everlasting God" (Brown/Riley), between the chorus and verse. Remember that if you have a bass player, you may not even need to play the left hand.

TRACK 75

This turn could work in "Forever" by Chris Tomlin (chorus to verse):

TRACK 76

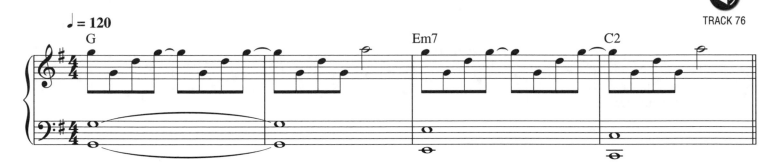

The previous example shows how a turn can incorporate a repeated pattern in the right hand over changing bass notes. (You could also just repeat the octave Gs in the left hand in bars 3 and 4.)

Here are two possible turns between verses of "Great Is Thy Faithfulness" (Chisholm/Runyan):

2-bar phrase

TRACK 77

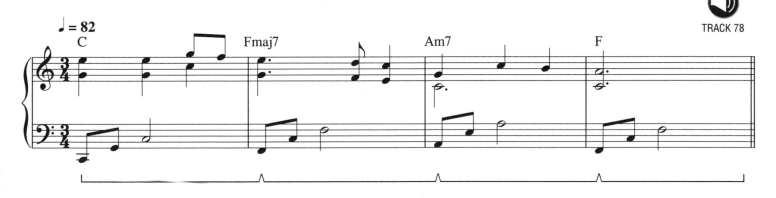

4-bar phrase

TRACK 78

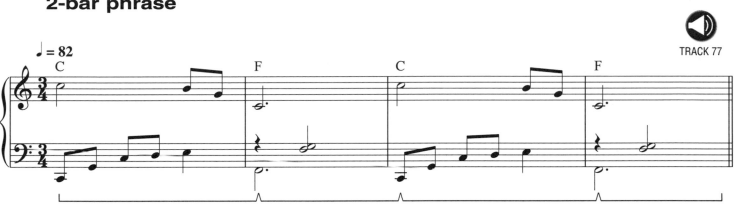

You could use this turn between the chorus and verse of "Our Great God" (Ortega/Powell):

TRACK 79

Here's a simpler version:

TRACK 80

Even simpler:

TRACK 81

How Long Should a Turn Be?

While some hymns don't need a turn between verses, most songs benefit from a turn of about four bars. There may be times, however, when a longer turnaround is appropriate. Reasons for lengthening a turn include: giving people more time to think about the lyrics they're singing, adding variety, or projecting a Scripture passage for people to read between sections of a song.

Don't assume that the turns played on a recording are the turns you should play. There are different factors that go into a recorded song (artistic creativity, featuring different instruments, etc.) that don't apply when leading a congregation.

 Choose three songs that you currently play in your church (or have been asked to play). Work out your own turns from chorus to verse, using some of the techniques we've covered in this book.

Chapter 18
ENDINGS

Note-reading pianists know a song has ended when there are no more notes, but playing worship songs by ear opens up a few more options. Let's take a look at them.

Play the turn again.

One common way to end a song is to play the turn once more, only this time it's called the "outro" or "tag." It generally ends on the tonic chord, although occasionally you might end a song on a 4 or 5 chord.

Play a single, arpeggiated chord.

An ending chord can be played once and held, or it can be stretched out by playing different notes of the chord. Here are three examples, all in the key of C. They should be played ad lib, with a slight ritard.

TRACK 82

Notice in the third example that, as you play higher in the register, you can use more color tones to add interest to the chord.

Slow down the last line.

Another common way to end the song is simply to play the last line (or a repeat of the last line) at a slower tempo. Here's what that might sound like in "O Great God" from Sovereign Grace Music:

TRACK 83

Play a prolonged, sustained chord.

At the end of a loud, exciting song, a congregation will sometimes want to applaud or shout (this is frowned upon in some churches). While it can be done in an overly emotionalistic way, if people's hearts are stirred by the truths of the gospel they've been singing, there's no better reason to make noise!

You can support that type of response by quickly alternating chords in the left and right hands, usually built on chords with a second added. This produces a rolling crescendo that can encourage a wholehearted response from the congregation.

Here's what it might look like written out:

TRACK 84

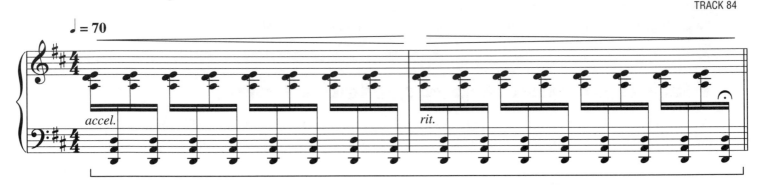

You can also play different triads in the right hand while holding the pedal down and repeating an octave in the left hand, like this:

TRACK 85

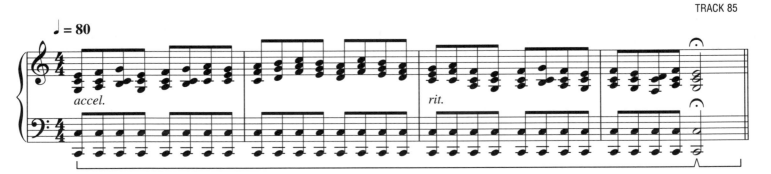

Of course, you can extend these patterns for as many measures as you'd like. The important thing is to support what a congregation wants to do or is already doing, rather than trying to manipulate a response musically. That's one reason why it's important to be able to hear the congregation whenever you're playing. You don't want to be getting louder on the keyboard as people are singing softer.

I should add that song endings can be both overrated and overused. Often the best place to end the song is when the lyrics are finished. Extended instrumental segments after the song is over can subtly communicate that church members are more spectators than participants. When the church gathers to sing, the primary focus should be the congregation's collective voice.

Chapter 19
TRANSITIONS

Guitarists who lead congregational worship often rely on the keyboardist to fill in the gaps between songs. This requires knowing how to play transitions well. Transitions are a lot like turns, except they're used between songs rather than sections of a song. They're not always needed, but they can be helpful when used judiciously and played well.

In modern settings, transitions are often handled by a sustained synth sound (usually open 5ths). We'll cover that in a later chapter.

Suppose your leader, who happens to be a guitarist, asks you to create a smooth musical flow from one song to another. This is easy if the songs are in the same key, time signature, and tempo. You can simply start the introduction of the new song on the last chord of the previous song.

That isn't always the way it works out, however. Sometimes you're transitioning to a song in the same tempo, but in a different key. In that case, you'll want to find the chords that lead into the new key (more on that in Chapter 23). For now, here's how that might sound going from "Jesus Paid It All" in A to an intro for "Come Behold the Wondrous Mystery" (Boswell/Papa/Bleecker) in E.

TRACK 86

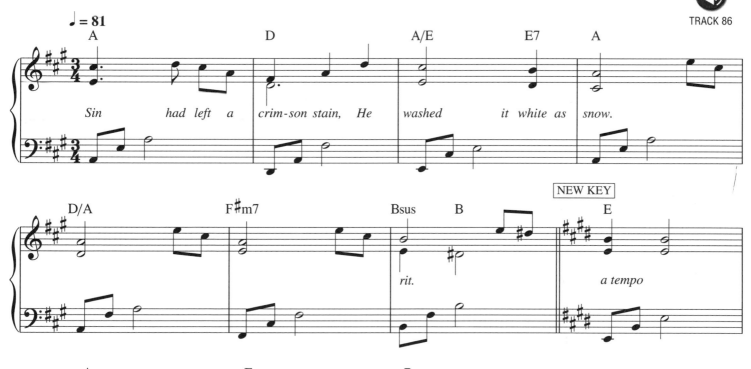

Now, let's suppose you're asked to transition to a song that's in a different key, different time signature, and different tempo. What then? No worries. You can start the introduction of the new song on the last chord of the old song, play it once in the old key, and then play it again in the new key.

Here's a sample transition between "It Is Well with My Soul" in the key of B♭ and "Before the Throne of God Above" (Cook/Bancroft) in the key of C:

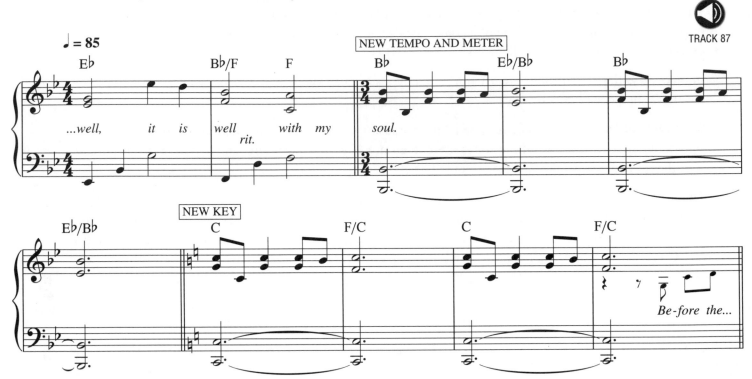

Notice that you're starting the tempo of the new song on the last sung note of the previous song. This creates a smooth transition that goes virtually unnoticed.

 See if you can work out seamless transitions between the following pairs of songs. Keep in mind that you'll sometimes want to slow down slightly at the end of the first song before starting the next song.

Same tempo, same key, same meter (D)

"In Christ Alone" (Getty/Townend) to "All I Have Is Christ" (Kauflin)

Same tempo, same meter, different key (E to C)

"10,000 Reasons" (Myrin/Redman) to "Cornerstone" (Myrin/Morgan/Liljero/Mote)

Different tempo, same meter, different key (G to E)

"This Is Amazing Grace" (Wickham/Farro/Riddle) to "10,000 Reasons" (Myrin/Redman)

The last pairing is the most difficult. Try slowing down at the end of the first song, and then play a few transitional chords in the tempo of the new song.

Chapter 20
INCORPORATING DYNAMICS

Playing the right notes at the right tempo and in the right key is important, but some keyboardists play everything at the same volume. It might be loud or soft, but there's little variation. That's why, along with harmony, rhythm and melody, the pianist's role is to add dynamics to the band's sound.

Dynamics help you shape a song in keeping with the emotion conveyed by the lyrics from chord to chord, section to section, and song to song. They also help you sound more musical than mechanical.

Finger to Finger

The first step to using dynamics effectively is realizing that when playing a chord, you don't have to play each finger with the same force. For instance, emphasizing the top note in a progression of chords makes the melody stand out and the chords sound more fluid.

When playing two notes, you can add weight to the upper note while playing the lower note lightly with the thumb. Try it with this progression in the keys of C and D:

TRACK 88

 Go back to the melody line you played for "10,000 Reasons" (page 43). Try playing it with more emphasis on the top melodic notes.

 On the next page, practice emphasizing the top notes in an arrangement of "When I Survey the Wondrous Cross."

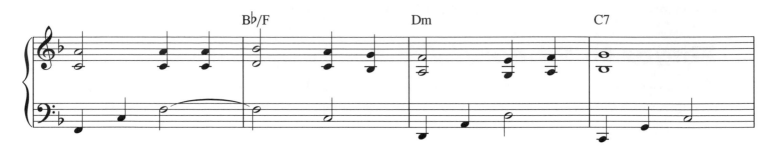

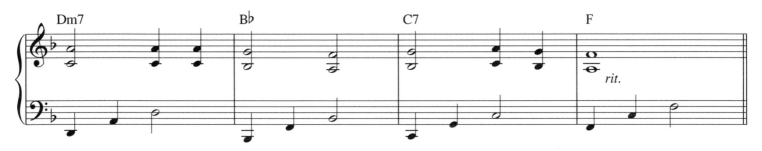

Chord to Chord

Chords don't have to be played at the same volume either. Give more weight to the chords marked with tenutos in the following exercise.

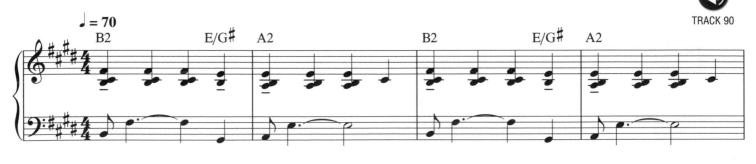

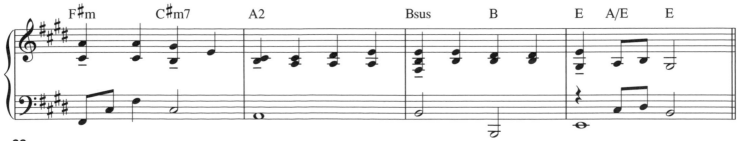

Section to Section

You can highlight different sections of a song by changing registers and dynamics at the same time. "In Christ Alone" is a beautiful modern hymn by Keith Getty and Stuart Townend. Over four verses, it covers a lot of theological and emotional ground. The third verse begins with a reference to Jesus' body in the tomb, one of the more reflective moments. At that point, it would serve the lyrics to bring the volume down and perhaps move to a higher area of the keyboard. You could even suggest changing to a minor harmony to better reflect the lyrics.

But in the middle of the verse, the mood shifts dramatically as we sing about Christ "bursting forth in glorious day" from the grave! This implies a change in the volume of the accompaniment. Here's an example of what you could do:

TRACK 91

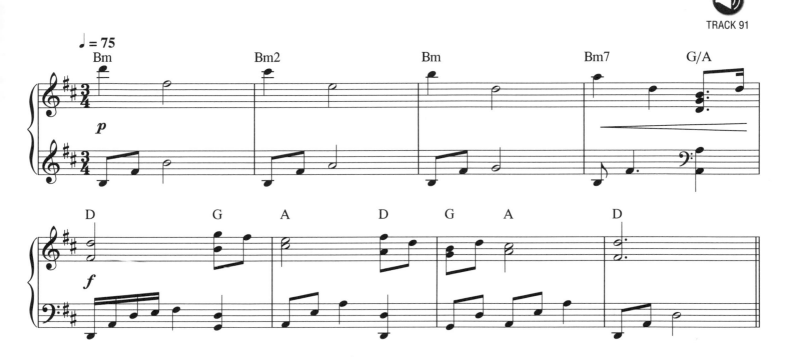

Shaping a Song

Everything we've talked about thus far regarding dynamics can be used to serve the larger purpose of mapping out a song. It's helpful to think through the lyrics in advance to determine what that might look like. Of course, every song doesn't require varying dynamics. Some songs are best suited for playing through at one consistent volume. But, when you have the opportunity, dynamics can deepen the impact of a song. Beginning on the next page, you'll find an example of what you might do with each verse of the moving hymn, "It Is Well with My Soul" (Spafford/Bliss). Keep in mind, this approach works best when playing with a small band or by yourself.

Verse 1 includes a reference to "peace like a river." So, we could begin with a simple accompaniment that suggests calm.

Verse 2 begins with the phrase, "Though Satan should buffet, though trials should come…" Here, we can use a little more movement to convey turmoil.

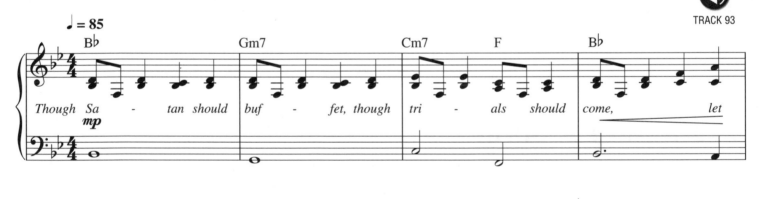

Verse 3 says, "My sin, O the bliss of this glorious thought; my sin, not in part, but the whole…" These are words to reflect upon, and minimizing movement in the keyboard facilitates that. As the realization of forgiveness sinks in, the left hand begins to move, expressing a welling up of emotion.

TRACK 94

Verse 4 speaks of awaiting the Lord's glorious return. We can build anticipation with repeated 8th notes in the left hand.

TRACK 95

 YOUR TURN Play the following songs, exploring different ways to shape each verse. Try to use what you've learned about dynamics from finger to finger and chord to chord as well.

- Amazing Grace

- In Christ Alone (Getty/Townend)

- When I Survey the Wondrous Cross (Tune: HAMBURG)

Chapter 21

PUTTING IT ALL TOGETHER

We've covered a number of principles for playing keyboard in a contemporary band, or as a soloist. It's difficult, though, to communicate how to do all these things musically. Here are a few miscellaneous points that will help you serve more effectively in either setting.

Think in musical phrases.

It's helpful to think of playing music like speaking. In order for a speech to be meaningful and effective, there will be moments of space to set off phrases, thoughts and sentences. Similarly, there are times in playing when it makes sense to stop a pattern to allow a song to breathe. Depending on the song, a pattern might need to change in the middle of a verse, at the end of a chorus, or somewhere else. Don't assume that once you start a pattern you have to keep it going. Sensitive musical phrasing comes through making small changes at transitions. Here's an example that could accompany the chorus of "Man of Sorrows" (Ligertwood/Crocker).

TRACK 96

Repeat chords.

A repeated chord, or inversions of a chord, can be used effectively for song sections that are supposed to build anticipation. Here's what that might sound like in a turn leading into the fourth verse of "In Christ Alone" (Getty/Townend).

TRACK 97

Repeated chords can also be effective when used over the normal chord changes of a song. Here's an example of what that might sound like in a verse of "All I Have Is Christ" by Jordan Kauflin.

TRACK 98

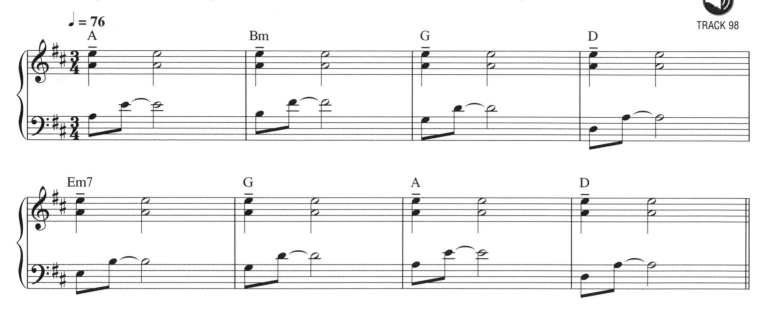

Use the pedal wisely.

We haven't talked much about using the sustain pedal, but it plays an important role. More often than not, pianists use the sustain pedal too much, due to insecurity or simply not listening. That habit muddies up what they're playing and minimizes any rhythmic elements they might be adding.

The lower you play on the keyboard, the more important it is to watch how much you're using the pedal. Play the following example with the pedal sustained throughout each line, and take note of the difference the register you're playing in makes.

TRACK 99

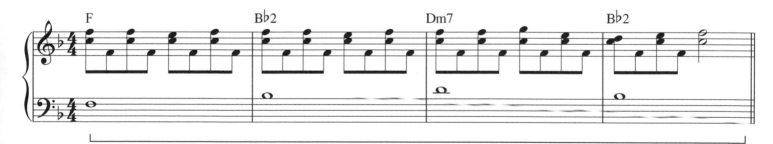

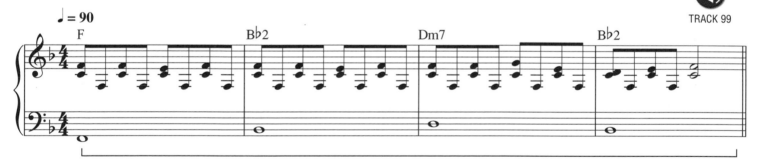

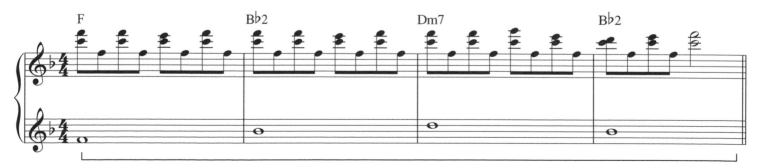

Play open chords with a few fills.

If you're playing with a band, most of your parts will be open chords with a few fills in between. Remember that other instruments are covering rhythmic and harmonic elements. Here's what you might play for the chorus of the Casting Crowns song "Glorious Day" (Hall/Bleecker):

TRACK 100

Again, where you play melodic fills will depend on what others in the band are playing. The above part should fit in most cases, although you could play your left hand higher, or not at all!

It's important to remember that your particular situation is unique. What you play will be affected by the size of your band, your leader, the skill level of the other musicians, what serves your congregation musically, your own experience, and other factors. Keep listening to the band as you play and seek input from musicians who are more familiar with contemporary styles.

 Take some of the songs that you've played in your church and apply what we've covered in this chapter to them. Figure out where you can improve your musical phrasing, use repeated chords, tighten up your use of the pedal, or play more sparsely.

Chapter 22

PLAYING BEHIND SOMEONE SPEAKING

Depending on the context, you might need to play an "underscore" behind someone who is praying, welcoming others, sharing a testimony, exhorting the congregation, or reading Scripture. If so, here are few things to avoid:

Music that's too loud

Obviously, this creates problems for those trying to focus on someone speaking. The fault might be on the person running the sound, rather than the keyboardist. Still, you shouldn't play anything bombastic when the congregation's attention should be on the speaker.

Music that's too creative or complex

Playing behind someone speaking isn't the best time to keep yourself musically stimulated, explore new harmonic progressions, try out strange melodic jumps, or wander aimlessly up and down the keyboard. Again, this can distract the congregation from the person speaking.

Music that's overly familiar

I know people mean well when they play a familiar song behind someone praying, but I often have to avoid a train wreck in my mind as the song lyrics collide with the words of the prayer. Occasionally this can work with the right song, but I wouldn't make it a regular practice.

Music that's played poorly or timidly

If you regularly hit wrong notes, or you're trying to figure out what to play as you go along, you're not serving the speaker or the congregation.

Music that's inappropriate

Hopefully it's obvious that you should avoid playing happy music behind a prayer of repentance, lethargic music behind a passionate proclamation, and busy music behind anything.

Here are some things I've found helpful to remember when playing underscores:

- Listen more to the speaker than to what you're playing.

- Allow spaces in what you're playing for the speaker to be heard.

- Play chord progressions that are relatively simple, brief and repetitive. Try using some of the turnarounds from Chapter 17. A short, repeated pattern will enable you to end it conveniently once the speaker is finished.

- It can be less distracting if you transition to the tempo and key of the next song while someone is speaking rather than after they're done.

- Play a non-rhythmic progression that reflects and supports the words being shared.

- Perhaps most importantly, don't assume you have to play anything at all. We should be comfortable with and even appreciate transitions and spoken words that stand on their own.

Melody or Harmony?

If you're playing something in rhythm, you have a choice between playing something that's melody-driven or harmony-driven. The choice is up to you.

Here are a few examples of simple patterns you could play as a brief underscore:

TRACK 101

TRACK 102

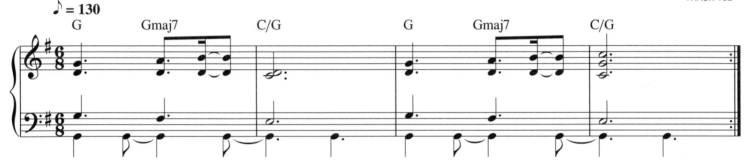

TRACK 103

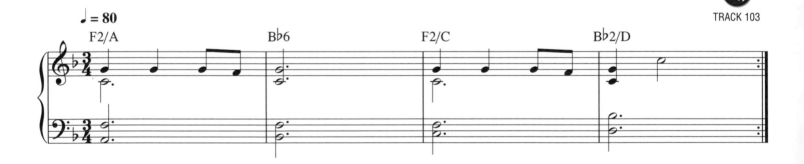

YOUR TURN Choose a song your church sings that's in 4/4 meter. Come up with a 2-bar phrase and a 4-bar phrase you could play as an underscore using the tempo and key of that song. Do the same thing for a 6/8 song and a 3/4 song.

Chapter 23

MODULATING

At times, you'll probably be asked to modulate (change keys) between songs or within a song. Don't panic! Every key can be connected to another key in some way. You just need to figure out how.

The Circle of 5ths

If you're not already familiar with the circle of 5ths, you're in for a treat. The circle of 5ths is used to describe the relationship between different keys. It's built on the understanding that a chord built on the fifth (dominant) note of any scale pulls us toward the tonic. When you're modulating, you want to create a natural "pull" toward the new key. That's why the circle of 5ths is important for modulations.

The circle of 5ths starts with the key of C at the top. If you go immediately to the right (clockwise), you'll find the dominant of C, which is G major. Keep going and you'll get to D major, which is the dominant of G, and so on.

If you go to the left from C, you'll reach F. Not surprisingly, C is the dominant of F. We won't worry about the key signatures because, hopefully, you already know those!

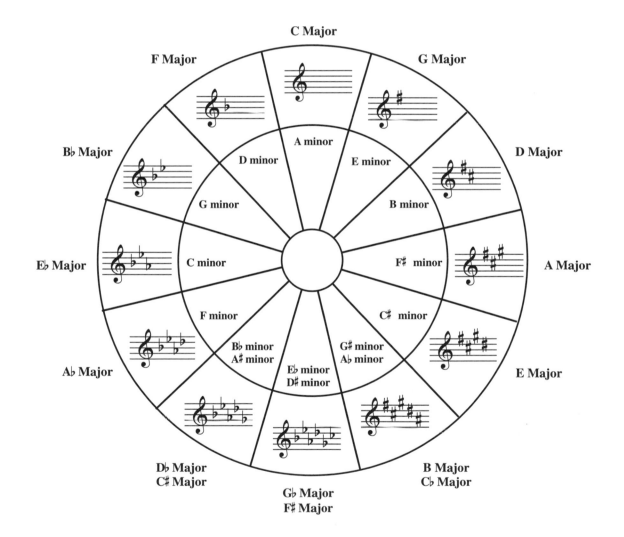

Notice that the relative minor keys are in the middle of the circle. They're often interchangeable with major chords in harmonic progressions.

Here's how the circle of 5ths can help with modulations. If you want to modulate to the key of D, for instance, all you need to do is play the dominant of D, which is A. That chord will naturally want to resolve to D. Try playing these examples using different inversions and voicings.

Whole-Step Modulations

From C to D:

1 (old key)	5 (new key)	1 (new key)
C	A	D

From F to G:

1 (old key)	5 (new key)	1 (new key)
F	D	G

When modulating, it's helpful to find chords and notes that are common to both the old and new key. This can be done with a "double dominant" slash chord. You can combine the dominant of the old key and the dominant of the new key by playing the dominant *chord* of the old key in the right hand and the dominant *root* of the new key in the left hand. If you're modulating from C to D, the double dominant chord would be G/A. From F to G, the double dominant chord would be C/D.

Confused yet? Try playing these examples:

1 (old key)	4/5 (new key)	1 (new key)
D	A/B	E
B♭	F/G	C

For an even stronger modulation, you can play the dominant of the new key after playing the double dominant chord. Here's what that looks like:

1 (old key)	4/5 (new key)	5 (new key)	1 (new key)
C	G/A	A	D
G	D/E	E	A

The double dominant (or 4/5) chord is helpful because it signals to the ear where the chords are heading.

Of course, the timing of the chords you play depends on the tempo, the meter of the song, and your personal preferences.

Half-Step Modulations

Things get a little trickier when you modulate by a half step. If you go straight to the 5 chord of the new key, it can sound a little "cheesy."

1 (old key)	5 (new key)	1 (new key)
A	F	B♭

Including the double dominant chord makes it slightly more palatable (as long as the voicing is thoughtful):

1 (old key)	4/5 (new key)	5 (new key)	1 (new key)
A	E♭/F	F	B♭

There are more options. Because the circle of 5ths sounds so natural to our ears, you can extend a modulation by moving further down the circle of 5ths, and then coming back to the new key. It's also possible to use a minor chord instead of a major chord. For example, here's a half-step modulation using the minor 2 chord of the new key.

1 (old key)	5 (old key)	♭3m/2m (old key/new key)	4/5 (new key)	1 (new key)
A	**E**	**Cm**	**E♭/F**	**B♭**

Minor Third Modulations

If you need to modulate a minor third, here's an example of what you might do:

1 (old key)	1m^7 (old key)	1/2 (new key)	2m^7 (new key)	5 (new key)	1 (new key)
E	**Em7**	**G/A**	**Am7**	**C/D**	**G**

When modulating, keep in mind that using chords and notes that are common to both keys will create a smoother transition. Here's how an inexperienced player might voice this progression:

TRACK 104

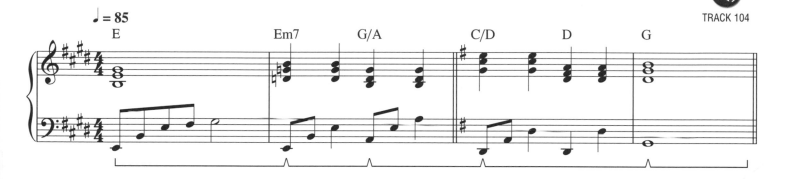

Not very appealing, is it? You can make it smoother and less noticeable by adding a melodic line:

TRACK 105

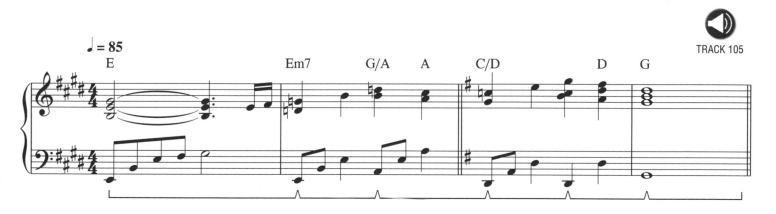

Notice a few things about this example. First, I didn't feel compelled to include every note in each chord. Second, I added some chords to make the progression smoother. Finally, I established a melodic line in measure 2 and repeated it in the next bar.

Also, notice the A chord at the end of measure 2. Remembering the circle of 5ths, an A chord could also lead us to a new key of D. But the melodic line provided a new "hook" for the ear to latch on to, so I was able to continue the harmonic changes and resolve to G. This brings us to the next modulation technique.

Repeat a Melody

Another way to modulate is to play a turn in the old key, and then play it again in the new key. This sends a very clear signal that you've changed keys. Here's what it would look like using the introduction for "Come, Thou Fount of Every Blessing" you've seen before:

TRACK 106

Abrupt or "Cold" Modulations

The last modulation technique we'll look at is simply to go straight to the new key with no warning. This approach could be used in the Sovereign Grace Music version of the hymn "All Creatures of Our God and King" between verses 3 and 4. It sounds like this:

TRACK 107

Keep in mind that this only works well if people are familiar with the arrangement (i.e. they expect the modulation), and the congregation can hear the band and vocals well enough to follow.

Chapter 24

ACOUSTIC PIANO VS. ELECTRONIC KEYBOARD

While the primary focus of this book has been to help you play the piano by ear, many readers use an electronic keyboard or synthesizer. They both have black and white keys, but that's where the similarities end. There are significant differences that affect what and how you play.

What an Acoustic Piano Can Do

If you're playing an acoustic piano, either an upright or a grand, the sound will have more natural overtones than an electronic keyboard. Electronic pianos have come a long way since the '70s, but they still haven't managed to emulate exactly the complex sound of multiple vibrating strings. This means an acoustic piano will fill a greater part of the audio spectrum, making the "less is more" principle even more important.

One advantage of playing an acoustic piano is that you're able to play with a greater degree of dynamics. Those dynamics won't always come out as clearly in a band context, but at specific moments (introductions, endings, or piano-only songs), an acoustic piano can be more expressive than its electronic cousin.

What an Acoustic Piano Can't Do

An acoustic piano can't give you access to multiple sounds. The world of synthesizers has grown exponentially in the past few decades. You can access literally thousands of different sounds through a combination of keyboard controllers, software programs, pedals, computers, and other gear.

This book can only barely introduce you to that world. If you'd like to invest more into that area, you can visit a variety of websites and Facebook groups. Your best option is to find someone trustworthy who can help you grow in your synth knowledge and skills.

What I want to suggest here is a basic list of sounds (or "patches") you should have if you're expected to play synth sounds:

Electric piano (Fender Rhodes, Wurlitzer, etc.)

This sounds similar to a piano, but has different, often warmer tones. Tremolo or phasing is added to deepen the sound, and certain patches have a bell-like quality. If you're playing with someone else who's playing piano, your use of this sound will be limited. Be careful not to steal the pianist's part!

If it's just you, this sound can be effective for quiet, intimate songs or sections. In other words, it wouldn't be ideal for a song like "This Is Amazing Grace," but it might fit very well on a laid-back version of "10,000 Reasons." You can play it as you would a normal piano, or focus on parts in the upper register. Be careful not to use the sustain pedal too much, however. Lifting the pedal at certain moments can make a part clearer and give it more personality.

Strings

Most synths have a myriad of string sounds to choose from. They're similar to the ambient sounds we'll talk about in a moment, but clearer and more defined. Generally, strings sound best when you use open voicings and keep note movement to a minimum. In other words, avoid playing triads. As a general rule, don't play more than three notes at a time, and stay in the upper registers. Good string patches can also be used to double a melodic line in the middle or upper registers.

The following example could be an appropriate string part for the chorus of Chris Tomlin's "Jesus Messiah" in the key of G. Notice that you don't even need your left hand.

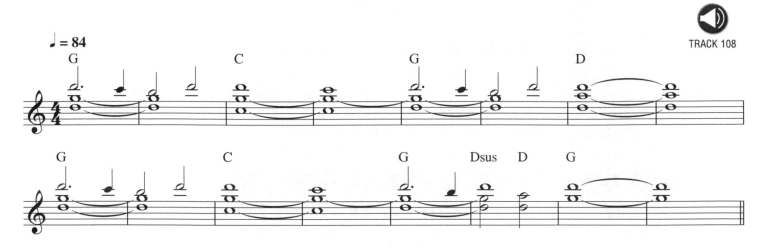

Organ

Playing the organ is a skill in itself. It has a long and varied history that we won't be able to discuss here. Similar to playing a string patch, organ sounds are typically played in the upper registers, with no more than three or four notes. You'll rarely need your left hand unless you're experienced in this genre.

Ambient sounds

Ambient sounds (pads, beds) are texture patches that help fill out a sound. They can also provide a musical background during transitions. Modern guitar players have developed this area significantly in recent decades. If you're in a band, be careful not to double what the electric guitarist is doing.

Like strings, ambient sounds sound best when you're using open chord voicings. The less movement, the better. Experiment with various patches played in different registers and make note of the ones you like.

When pianists discover ambient sounds, they often overuse them. In fact, that can be the case with any new sound! Remember that what you *don't* play is just as important as what you *do* play. If you find that you're playing every section of every song, you're playing too much. Listen to the rest of the band and determine where your part is *needed*.

Bells

You'll typically play bell sounds in the upper register to accent certain chords or melodic motifs. Bells are like strong spices—if used too much, they become overbearing. Bells tend to work best as either single notes or octaves.

Sequenced sounds

Sequenced sounds are beyond the scope of this book, but are commonplace in many of today's worship bands. If you're interested in learning more about them, check out sites like www.loopcommunity.com, the Omnisphere Facebook page, and user groups for Ableton, Reason and Logic.

If You're Buying a Synth

Synthesizers come in all shapes and sizes. You don't even have to purchase a full synthesizer, per se. Many players use a keyboard controller with sounds produced through programs like Ableton, Reason and Logic. Here are some general tips:

Do your research.

Ask friends, visit music stores, browse websites and online reviews. Visit sites like www.sweetwater.com and www.guitarcenter.com to see what's available. Don't buy an instrument without checking it out first.

Establish your budget in advance.

Whatever you have to spend, you'll most likely find something that will meet your needs. The higher-end synthesizers can do more and have better sounds, but synths have come a long way in recent decades.

Don't buy more than you'll use.

Like computers, synthesizers can do thousands of things that most users never benefit from. If you're just getting started, look for a simpler layout. On the other hand, if you're eager to grow in this area, challenge yourself. Just make sure you don't buy something so overwhelming that you end up using the same six sounds anyway.

Consider getting a controller to use with software.

If you're serious about growing in this area, consider purchasing a keyboard controller to trigger sounds from your computer. You won't be limited by the sounds contained in your synthesizer, and you can keep up with new technology.

Explore your sounds.

Synthesizers usually come preloaded with anywhere from 100 to 2000 sounds, or more. Take time to listen to as many as you can, making note of the ones you think might possibly serve your church well. It's a good idea to jot down what's unique about the sounds that you like.

Create a cheat sheet.

Unless your synthesizer is very basic, write up a quick reference chart for where your most-used sounds are stored. That way, you won't have to figure it out on the fly.

Chapter 25
PRACTICING

We've finally come to the most important part of the book. Really. No one learns anything by simply receiving information. We have to put it into practice. Hopefully, you've been doing that as you've worked your way through this book. If so, you should be quite a bit more comfortable with chord charts than you were when you started.

When I was in college, I remember certain students who spent hours with their instrument, but never seemed to get much better. It's a sad fact that you can practice a long time and have nothing to show for it.

What's the secret?

Practice the right way.

In his book, *Talent Is Overrated*[1], Geoff Colvin highlights five qualities of effective practicing:

It's designed to improve performance.

Practicing is more than simply playing what you know. Good practice habits make you better than you were. That means you should target your weaknesses—the gaps in your skills—rather than what you're comfortable with.

It has a high degree of repetition.

I don't remember where I first heard it, but one of my favorite quotes about practicing is:

> *Don't practice until you get it right. Practice until you can't get it wrong.*

Getting something right once might be a complete accident, but we often walk away feeling confident that we'll play it correctly from then on. What we find is that, in another setting at another time, we quickly return to old habits. If we're going to learn anything well, we have to play it dozens, maybe even hundreds of times for it to stick. That's what I mean by a high degree of repetition.

There is immediate, measurable feedback.

The fruit of good practicing can be seen right away. Too often we stumble through a new concept or technique and think we've "learned" it. No, we've just stumbled through it. We need to practice chord voicings, inversions, playing less, etc. until we can see and hear the difference.

It's mentally challenging.

Good practicing makes you think. You can certainly learn a great deal just through rote repetition. But it's your mind that will enable you to understand the relationship between chords, notice patterns you didn't see before, and use your newfound skills in a sensitive way.

---

[1] Geoff Colvin, *Talent Is Overrated: What Really Separates World-Class Performers from Everybody Else* (Penguin Publishing Group, 2010), 65-83.

It requires hard work.

You probably saw this one coming. Practicing is not for the faint of heart. It's really hard, in spite of the people who advertise they can teach you to play by ear in ten easy lessons. They might be the best lessons in the world, but if you don't do the hard work of practice, you'll never get better. Here's the good news. If you remember that your goal is to serve your church in a greater variety of ways, and that in so doing, the people will more deeply appreciate how good, glorious and great God is, it will be a joy to practice.

Use a metronome.

As you start thinking about chord voicings and creative musical ideas, it's easy to lose track of the tempo. Your band really won't appreciate that. Neither will the members of your church. That's why it's a good idea to use a metronome when you're practicing these exercises. Slow it down so you can play it correctly. Give yourself enough time to think about what you're going to play.

Listen.

One of the best ways to grow in knowing what to play is by listening to pianists on recordings, especially recordings of the songs that you're being asked to play on Sundays (see page 86 for suggestions). You'll probably be surprised how little the piano is actually used. That's just another reminder that **less is more**.

Another way to benefit from listening is to play along with recordings, adding parts that you think are appropriate. Don't assume that everything you're playing is stellar, but it's a great way to develop your listening skills outside the Sunday morning context.

Practice with others.

Practicing alone can bring untold benefits. What it *can't* do is simulate the actual experience of playing with others in a live situation. Ask a few friends to join you on a Saturday morning to go through some of the songs you play at your church. Ask for their feedback on what works and what doesn't. It may be a humbling experience, but we're told in James 4:6 that "God opposes the proud but gives grace to the humble" (ESV). More grace means that you'll actually get better at playing by ear!

CONCLUSION

If you've been faithful in working through the "Your Turn" exercises in this book, I trust that you're much more confident using chord charts than you were when you started.

But don't stop now! Keep exploring how God might want to use your musical talents to serve His people. The greatest joy lies not in simply mastering a new skill, but in knowing that God is working through you to draw people's attention to the Savior who "bore our sins in his body on the tree, that we might die to sin and live to righteousness" (1 Peter 2:24, ESV). We have no better reason to sing, and no better reason to play.

LISTENING LIST

Here are some albums and songs that reflect the content of this book:

Piano Only

Sovereign Grace Music:
Together for the Gospel Live
>> In Christ Alone
>> It Is Well with My Soul

Sovereign Grace Music:
Together for the Gospel Live II
>> All I Have Is Christ
>> Holy, Holy, Holy
>> Jesus Paid It All
>> Praise to the Lord, the Almighty
>> When I Survey

Sovereign Grace Music:
Together for the Gospel Live III
>> Be Thou My Vision
>> Come Behold the Wondrous Mystery
>> He Will Hold Me Fast
>> His Forever

Fernando Ortega: *Hymns & Meditations*
>> Come Thou Fount
>> Nothing But the Blood
>> What Wondrous Love Is This?

Piano with Band

Matt Redman: *10,000 Reasons*
>> Holy
>> 10,000 Reasons (Bless the Lord)

Chris Tomlin: *Never Lose Sight*
>> Jesus

Crowder: *Neon Steeple*
>> Come as You Are

All Sons & Daughters: *All Sons & Daughters*
>> Great Are You Lord

Hillsong Worship: *Open Heaven / River Wild*
>> O Praise the Name (Anástasis)

Keith & Kristyn Getty: *Facing a Task Unfinished*
>> The Lord Is My Salvation
>> My Worth Is Not in What I Own

Elevation Worship: *Here as in Heaven*
>> Here as in Heaven
>> O Come to the Altar
>> Resurrecting

Sovereign Grace Music: *The Gathering*
>> Now Why This Fear
>> Shine into Our Night

Norton Hall: *Be Thou My Vision*
>> Nothing But the Blood of Jesus

Matt Boswell: *Messenger Hymns, Vol. 1*
>> To the Cross I Cling